Japanese Short Stories for Complete Beginners

30 Exciting Short Stories to Learn Japanese & Grow Your Vocabulary the Fun Way

©All rights reserved 2019
Frédéric BIBARD (TalkInJapanese.com)

No part of this book including the audio material may be copied, reproduced, transmitted or distributed in any form without prior written permission of the author. For permission requests, write to: Frédéric BIBARD at contact@talkinjapanese.com.

For more products by Frédéric BIBARD, visit

https://www.amazon.com/Frederic-BIBARD (for US)

https://www.amazon.co.uk/Frederic-BIBARD (for UK)

or go to https://talkinjapanese.com.

Table Of Contentents

はじめに 7
Introduction 7
ハンズフリー版をご希望ですか? 9
Want The Hands-Free Version? 9
第1話：初日 - パート1 10
Story 1 : First Day - Part 1 10
第2話：初日 - パート2 13
Story 2 : First Day - Part 2 13
第3話：初日 - パート3 15
Story 3 : First Day - Part 3 15
第4話：休暇に出かける - パート1 17
Story 4 : Going On Holiday – Part 1 17
第5話：休暇に出かける - パート2 19
Story 5 : Going On Holiday – Part 2 19
第6話：海外での食料品の買い物 21
Story 6 : Food Shopping Abroad 21
第7話：休暇の忙しい一日 (1) 23
Story 7 : A Busy Day In The Holidays (1) 23
第8話：チョコレートケーキ 26
Story 8 : Chocolate Cake 26
第9話：スコーンの焼き方 29
Story 9 : How To Bake Scones 29
第10話：インターネット 32
Story 10 : Internet 32
第11話：チャネル・トンネル 34
Story 11 : Channel Tunnel 34
第12話：天気予報 37
Story 12 : Weather Report 37
第13話：休暇の忙しい一日 (2) 39
Story 13 : A Busy Day In The Holidays (2) 39
第14話：スマートフォン 41

Story 14 : Smartphones 41

第15話：チェスター 43
Story 15 : Chester 43

第16話：家族の休日 - パート1 45
Story 16 : A Family Holiday – Part 1 45

第17話：家族の休日 - パート2 47
Story 17 : A Family Holiday – Part 2 47

第18話：家族の休日 - パート3 49
Story 18 : A Family Holiday – Part 3 49

第19話：家族の休日 - パート4 51
Story 19 : A Family Holiday – Part 4 51

第20話：家族の休日 - パート5 53
Story 20 : A Family Holiday – Part 5 53

第21話：家に帰る 55
Story 21 : Getting Home 55

第22話：買い物とランチ(1) 58
Story 22 : Out Shopping And For Lunch (1) 58

第23話：買い物とランチ(2) 60
Story 23 : Out Shopping And For Lunch (2) 60

第24話：買い物とランチ(3) 62
Story 24 : Out Shopping And For Lunch (3) 62

第25話：休暇の終わり(1) 64
Story 25 : End Of The Holidays (1) 64

第26話：休暇の終わり(2) 66
Story 26 : End Of The Holidays (2) 66

第27話：休暇の終わり(3) 71
Story 27 : End Of The Holidays (3) 71

第28話：休暇の終わり(4) 73
Story 28 : End Of The Holidays (4) 73

第29話：休暇の終わり(5) 75
Story 29 : End Of The Holidays (5) 75

第30話：休暇の終わり(6) 77
Story 30 : End Of The Holidays (6) 77

結論 80
Conclusion 80
音声をダウンロードする方法に関する説明 81
Instructions On How To Download The Audio 81
About Talk In Japanese 82
Talk In Japaneseについて 82

はじめに

INTRODUCTION

Everybody loves stories. I'm sure you do, too. So how would you like to learn Japanese with the help of very short stories? It's fun and easy!

Most students who learn Japanese as a second language say they are having the most trouble with the following issues:

Lack of vocabulary

Difficulty in picking up grammar structures, and

Hesitation in speaking Japanese because of (1) pronunciation troubles or (2) listening comprehension problems.

This collection of 30 very short stories will help you solve those challenges. At only 300 words per story, this book is created for complete beginners with little to no previous experience in learning Japanese.

Learn new vocabulary

The stories in this book are written using the most useful Japanese words. After each story, you will find a list of vocabulary used in the story together with its Japanese translation. There is no need to reach for a dictionary each time you encounter words you don't understand, and you will quickly learn new words as you go along.

Easily grasp Japanese sentence structures

Written with a good mix of descriptive sentences and simple dialogue, the stories will introduce you to different types of sentence structures. This way, you'll be able to naturally pick up English grammar structures as you read the stories.

Practice your listening comprehension

To be able to speak Japaneses well, you need to expose your ears to a lot of spoken Japanese. You can do that by listening to the free audio narration of the stories. Listen to the words out loud and compare them to the written stories. Read along to the narration. Copy the correct pronunciation and practice the inflections. With enough practice, you will soon be able to get over your hesitations in speaking Japanese.

Learning Japanese as a second language can be a scary task. But with these short stories, you can make it as fun and as easy as possible. Before you know it, you have already learned hundreds of new Japanese words, exposed yourself to a variety of sentence structures, and listened to enough spoken English that your pronunciation will improve greatly.

So go ahead. Start reading and have some fun!

Best of luck!

Talk In Japanese Team

ハンズフリー版をご希望ですか?
WANT THE HANDS-FREE VERSION?

If you would like a hands-free and purely auditory way to listen to Japanese Short Stories for Complete Beginners, check out the audio version in Audible. The audiobook provides you with almost 3 hours of stories, vocabulary, glossary---all of it and more--all in pure audio.

Listen to the stories while driving your car, enjoy it in your commute, while doing your chores or on your morning run. Anywhere you go and whatever you do, your Audible version of the book goes with you.

第1話：初日 - パート1

STORY 1: FIRST DAY - PART 1

IMPORTANT: The link to download the MP3 is available at the end of this book (page 81).

アラームは07:00に設定されていますが、私は早く起きます。6時30分です。私は興奮していて、同時に緊張もしています。

The alarm is set for 0700 but I wake up early. It is 6.30. I am excited and nervous at the same time.

月曜日で、今日は私の新しい仕事を始める日です。

It's Monday and today is the day I start my new job.

私は起きてシャワーを浴びます。それから朝食を食べます。お腹がすいていませんが、コーヒーを飲みバナナを食べます。私は自分の昼食のサンドイッチを作ります。

I get up and take a shower. Then I have breakfast. I am not hungry but drink some coffee and eat a banana. I make myself a sandwich for my lunch.

私は着替えに行きます。おしゃれなスーツとブラウスを選びます。鏡を見ます。フォーマルすぎるように見えるので、気が変わります。濃い色のドレスとそれにマッチするジャケットはもっと気楽に感じると思います。

I go to get dressed. I choose a smart suit and blouse. I look in the mirror. I think I look too formal and change my mind. I find a dark coloured dress and matching jacket and feel much more comfortable.

私は歯を磨いて化粧をします。

I clean my teeth and put on some make-up.

私は自分の車の鍵を見つけてから時間を調べて、とても早いということに気づきます。7時15分です。そして、私は8時30分に仕事を始めます！

I find my car keys and then check the time, and realise that I am very early. It is 7.15 and I start work at 0830!

現時点で交通状況がどのようなものであるかわからないので、とにかく出発することにします。私はピーターとヘンリーに別れを告げます。

I decide to leave anyway as I don't know what the traffic is like at this time. I say goodbye to Peter and Henry.

第1話：初日 - パート1　　　　　　　　　　　　　　　　　　　　　STORY 1 : FIRST DAY - PART 1

私はちょうどいい時間、8時頃に到着し、車を駐車場に駐車し、そして新しい事務所のドアへ行きます。そこまで歩いて3分かかります。

I arrive in good time, at about 0800, park my car in the car park, and make my way to the door of my new office. It takes me 3 minutes to walk there.

私はドアをノックします。私の上司、ジャネットがドアに来て私を入れてくれます。

I knock on the door. My boss, Janet, comes to the door and lets me in.

すでに働いている人もいますし、彼女は私を新しい同僚に紹介します。彼女はこう言います。「こちらはサラさんです。彼女は新しい業務マネージャーです。」

Some people are already working and she introduces me to my new colleagues. She says, "This is Sarah. She's the new office manager".

私が彼らに紹介されるとき、誰もがとても親切で、「こんにちは」、「やあ」、「よろしくお願いします」と言います。

Everybody is very friendly and they say "Hello", "Hi" and "Pleased to meet you," as I am introduced to them.

ジャネットはトイレ、キッチンがどこにあるかを教えてくれ、それから彼女は私のデスクに案内してくれます。私は仕事を始めようと座ります。

Janet shows me where the toilets are, and the kitchen, then she shows me to my desk. I sit down to start work.

私には学ぶべきことがたくさんあり、とても早く朝が過ぎます。

I have a lot to learn and the morning passes very quickly.

間もなく昼休みです。私はサンドイッチを食べ、コーヒーを飲むために台所に行くことにします。

Before long, it is lunchtime. I decide to go to the kitchen to eat my sandwich and make some coffee.

私はかばんを開けて中を見ます。

I open my bag and I look inside.

私はかばんを空にします。取り出したものすべてを見てみます。私のサンドイッチはどこ？

I empty out my bag. I look at everything I have taken out. Where is the sandwich?

もう一度見ます。それでもサンドイッチはありません。

I look again. Still there is no sandwich.

しかたなく昼食にコーヒーだけを飲みます。

Just coffee for lunch then.

第2話：初日 - パート2

STORY 2 : FIRST DAY - PART 2

IMPORTANT: The link to download the MP3 is available at the end of this book (page 81).

私は社員用のキッチンでコーヒーを飲みながら座って電話のメッセージを見ます。たくさんの友達が私の新しい仕事の初日のために「頑張って」というメッセージを送っています。

I sit with my coffee in the staff kitchen and look at my phone messages. Lots of friends are sending me "good luck" messages for my first day in my new job.

私の同僚が、一人二人とキッチンに入ってきます。そして、彼らは皆フレンドリーで、こんにちはと言います。彼らは私が座っているところにやって来て、私と昼食を一緒に取ることにします。

My colleagues start to come into the kitchen in ones and twos and they are all friendly and say hello. They come over to where I am sitting and join me with their lunch.

彼らは私のことについて、どこに住んでいるか、恋人がいるかどうか、他にどんな仕事をしてきたのか、など私に質問します。

They ask me questions about myself, where I live, if I'm in a relationship, what other jobs I have done, and so on.

そして、答えはこちらです。

So, here are the answers:

私の名前はサラで、38歳です。

My name is Sarah and I am 38 years old.

私はスリムブリッジに住んでいます。スリムブリッジはオフィスから25キロほど離れた小さな村です。そこには約150軒の家、パブ、郵便局、新聞販売店、そして食料品店があります。教会は村の中心にあり、サッカー場とテニスコートがある公園があり、そこにはすべての子供たちが遊びに行きます。

I live in Slimbridge which is a small village about 25 kms away from the office. There are about 150 houses there, a pub, a post office and newsagent, and a grocery store. The church is at the centre of the village and there is a park with football pitches and tennis courts where all the children go to play.

私は11年間教師であるピーターと結婚しています、そして私たちには8歳の息子のヘンリーがいます。ヘンリーは元気いっぱいで、わんぱくです。私たちはみんなスポーツ

をするのが好きで、ヘンリーは村のサッカーチームに所属しています。彼は土曜日の朝に試合をします。そして、ピーターと私は出来るときは一緒に手伝いに行きます。

I have been married to Peter, a teacher, for 11 years and we have a son, Henry, who is 8 years old. Henry is full of energy and wants to be busy. We all like to do sport and Henry is in the village football team. He plays matches on a Saturday morning, and Peter and I go along to help when we can.

夫と私は冬の間はバドミントン、夏の間はテニスをします。私たちはできる限り頻繁にヘンリーと泳ぎに行きます。

My husband and I play badminton in the winter months and tennis during the summer. We go swimming with Henry as often as we can.

私の仕事はすべて、管理に関わっており、オフィスで仕事をします。私は事務処理が得意で、とても計画的に仕事をします。私は管理部門の仕事をしながら5年間銀行に勤め、ヘンリーが生まれたときに退職しました。

All of my jobs have involved administration and working in an office. I am good at paperwork and am very organised. I worked for a bank for five years, managing a department, and left there when Henry was born.

今、彼らは私についてよく知っています。

So now they know me better.

昼休みが終わり、私たち全員がおしゃべりをしながら笑顔でオフィスに戻ります。

The lunch break ends and we all go back to the office chatting and smiling.

第3話 : 初日 - パート3

STORY 3 : FIRST DAY - PART 3

IMPORTANT: The link to download the MP3 is available at the end of this book (page 81).

仕事の時間が終わり、私は帰路について考えます。17時30分です。

The working day comes to an end and I think about my journey home. It is 1730.

私は皆が出るのを待ってそれから、バッグを持ち、そしてオフィスの鍵を取り出します。私はオフィスの責任者を務めているので、オフィスを閉めて毎朝開ける責任があります。だから、私は朝、最初に到着する必要があります。

I wait for everybody to leave then pick up my bag and take out the office keys. I am responsible for locking the office, and opening it each morning, now that I am the office manager. So, I need to arrive first in the morning.

セキュリティアラームをセットし、窓をチェックします。そして私はコンピュータの電源が切れていることを確認しなければなりません。私はそれをすべてやり終えるのに15分ほどかかります。明日はもっと早くできるでしょう。

There is a security alarm to set as well as windows to check. And I must make sure the computers have been switched off. I do all of that and it takes me about 15 minutes. I'm sure I will be quicker tomorrow.

車を運転していると渋滞にはまります。25キロ運転して家に帰るのに1時間以上かかります。私は18時45分に家に着きます。

I drive away in my car and join a traffic jam. It takes me more than an hour to drive the 25 kms home. I get home at 1845.

私は車ではなく電車やバスで通勤することをゆっくり運転しながら考えます。

I spend the slow driving thinking about travelling by train or by bus instead of by car.

これらが私の選択肢です。

These are my options:

私の家からバス停まで徒歩わずか5分で、バスは毎時15分過ぎに1回運行しています。乗車時間は一時間です。バス停で降り、15分歩いて行きます。私が7時15分にバスに乗るとしたら、今朝より5分早く、7時10分までに家を出るでしょう。私は8時30分にオフィスに着くと思います。8時30分から仕事を始めるのでそれは厳しいです。

The bus stop is only 5 minutes' walk from my house and the buses run once per hour at a quarter past. The journey takes a full hour. When I get off at the bus station, I have a 15-minute walk ahead of me. If I take the bus at 0715, I will leave the house by 0710, 5 minutes earlier than this morning. I think I will arrive at the office at 0830. That's tight as I start work at 0830.

電車の駅は自宅から車で10分、そこにはほとんど駐車場がありません。電車は30分ごとに毎時5分と35分に運行しています。所要時間は25分です。駅から私のオフィスまでは徒歩10分です。電車に乗るには、7時15分に家を出る必要があります - 確実に駐車できるようにし、プラットフォームに着くために - 7時35分に電車に乗車します。私は8時に電車を降り、8時10分にオフィスに着くことができます。

The train station is a 10-minute drive from home and there is little parking there. The trains run every half hour at 5 and 35 minutes past each hour. The journey takes 25 minutes. The walk from the station to my office is 10 minutes. To take the train, I need to leave home at 0715 – to be sure to be able to park, and to get to the platform – for the train at 0735. I get off the train at 0800 and can be at the office for 0810.

家に着いたら、バスでの移動と電車での移動の料金を調べます。私は、車での移動にかかる費用、つまりガソリンの料金だけでなく駐車場の料金も比較します。

When I get home, I check the cost of travelling by bus and travelling by train. I compare the costs with travelling by car - paying for the car park as well as the cost of the petrol.

費用に関係なく、私は便利さがもっと重要であると思います。なので、私は車で通勤することを続けます。

Regardless of the cost, I decide that convenience is more important and I will continue to travel by car.

第4話：休暇に出かける - パート1

STORY 4 : GOING ON HOLIDAY – PART 1

IMPORTANT: The link to download the MP3 is available at the end of this book (page 81).

あなたが休暇を計画しているときに考えることがたくさんあります。

There is a lot to think about when you are planning a holiday.

まず、どこに行くかを決める必要があります。目的地は頭の中にありますか？ あなたにはなにか目的地のアイデアがあるかもしれません、またないかもしれません。

Firstly, you need to decide where to go. Do you have a destination in mind? You may have, but you may not.

あなたはアクティブな休暇、または違った文化や言語について学ぶための休暇に行きたいかもしれません。またはプールのそばやビーチに横になって休日の間リラックスする以外何もしたくないかもしれません。または3つすべてを休暇に組み合わせて過ごしたいかもしれません。

You may want to go on an activity holiday, or perhaps a holiday to learn about a different culture or language, or you may want to lie by a pool or on a beach and do nothing but relax for the duration of your holiday. Or perhaps a combination of all 3.

あなたはあなたの時間をどのように過ごしたいかについて決める必要があります。

You have to decide on how you want to spend your time.

そして、特にあなたとあなたのパートナーがどこへ行くのか、何をするのかについて合意できない場合は、誰と一緒に行くかを決める必要があるかもしれません。

And you may also have to decide who to go with, especially if you and your travel party can't agree on where you're going or what you're doing.

現実には、あなたの選択肢はほぼ無限大ですが、しかし、下されるべき決定もまた無限大です。インターネットを使用すると、幅広い範囲のアイデア、目的地、そしてアクティビティを検討し、かつてないほど冒険的なことができます。

In reality, your options are almost endless, but so are the decisions to be made. The Internet enables you to consider a vast range of ideas, destinations and activities, and to be more adventurous than it has ever been possible to be.

そのための手順は次のとおりです：

So here are the steps to take:

1. **あなたが誰と一緒に行くつもりなのかを決める。**

1. Decide who you are going to go away with.

2. **予算に合致する。**

2. Agree your budget .

3. **あなたたち二人（または全員）が出かけることが出来る日を決める。**

3. Agree dates when you are both (or all) able to get away.

4. **あなたがどのように時間を過ごしたいのかを話し合う －せわしなく、アクティブに、啓発的に、のんびりする、または完全に他の何かをする。またはそれらすべてを合わせたもの。すべてに同意できない場合は、しばらくの間「自分の好きなことをする」ことに決めるでしょう。**

4. Discuss how you want to spend your time away – being busy, being active, being cultured, being lazy, or being something else altogether. Or a combination of them all. If you can't agree on everything, perhaps agree to 'do your own thing' for some of the time.

5. **滞在したい場所について少し話す時間を費やす：キャンプ？ ホテルや別荘で？ 家族と一緒に？ 星空の下で？**

5. Spend a little time talking about where you want to stay: camping? In a hotel or villa? With a family? Under the stars?

6. **休暇全体を自分で計画するのか、それとも旅行代理店に手伝ってもらうのかを検討する。**

6. Consider if you want to plan the entire holiday yourselves, or whether you welcome the help of a travel agent.

7. **国を選択して、それから実際の目的地または行き先、そしてキーとなるアクティビティを絞り込む。**

7. Agree your country, then narrow it down to your actual destination or destinations, and the key activities.

これで準備が整いました。実際にこれを実現する方法について考えてみましょう。

Now that you've got this far, let's think about how we actually make this happen.

第5話：休暇に出かける - パート2

STORY 5 : GOING ON HOLIDAY – PART 2

IMPORTANT: The link to download the MP3 is available at the end of this book (page 81).

あなたが休暇をとるときには、考慮すべきことがたくさんあります。それはストレスになる可能性がありますが、あなたが几帳面であるならば、そんなことはありません。

We know there is a lot to think about when you're going on holiday. It can be stressful, but it isn't if you're well-organised.

これで、誰といつ一緒に行くのかがわかります。あなたがどれだけ過ごしたいか、あるいは過ごせるか、どこにいたいのか、そして休暇中に何をしたいのか自分でわかっています。あなたはまた目的地を知っています。それは間違いなくなされるべき最も重要な決断です。

By now, you know who you're going with, and when. You know how much you want to spend or are able to spend, where you want to stay and what you want to do while you're away. You also know your destination, which is arguably the most important decision to be made.

旅行代理店の助けを借りずに、自分で手配して予約したとしましょう。この方法でコストは低くなりますが、リスクが高くなることがあるため、簡単な判断ではありません。

Let's assume that you're arranging and booking this yourself, without the help of a travel agent. You will find the costs are lower this way, but the risks are sometimes higher, so it isn't be an easy decision.

以下のアドバイスと手順は、作業を簡単にするでしょう。

The following advice and steps will make things easier:

1. **信頼している良い航空会社を選択する。希望の日程の空席状況を確認する。**

1. Choose a good airline that you have confidence in. Check availability of flights for the dates you want to travel.

2. **滞在する場所を探す。希望の日程の空室状況を確認する。何が含まれているのか、何が別料金なのかを考える。**

2. Look up places to stay. Check availability of accommodation for the dates you want to be away. Think about what is included and what is extra.

3. **どんなアクティビティが休暇の間にやりたいことと一致するかチェックする。**

3. Check out which activities match those you want to do while you are away.

4. すべてが一致したら、日付をもう一度確認して、フライトを予約する。おそらく複数の場所に滞在する必要があるが、自分に合ったフライトは1つしかないので、まず最初にフライトを予約する。

4. If everything matches up, check your dates again, then book your flights. You probably have more than one place to stay but there is probably only one flight that suits you, so book your flights first.

5. それから日付をもう一度確認し、宿泊施設を予約する。

5. Then check your dates again, and book your accommodation.

6. そして今、アクティビティを予約することを計画する。する前に、どれがあなたにとって最も重要であるかを決める。各アクティビティ提供者が提供する保険を見て、彼らが真剣に安全を考えてくれるかを確認する。

6. And now plan to book your activities. Before you do, decide which are the most important to you. Look at the insurance each activity provider offers and make sure they take your safety seriously.

7. もう一度日付を確認してから、先に進んでアクティビティを予約する。

7. Now, check your dates again, then go ahead and book your activities.

8. そして最後に、すぐに旅行保険に加入する。それがフライト、宿泊施設、医療ニーズ、そしてすべての持ち物を確実にカバーすることを確認する。あなたがどれだけの支出をしているかについて考えて、すべてがカバーされていることを確認する。

8. And finally, take out travel insurance straightaway. Make sure it covers you for your flights, accommodation, medical needs, and all your belongings. Think about how much you are spending and make sure everything is covered.

すべてに関して、領収書は安全な場所に保管しましょう。

With everything, keep your receipts in a safe place.

そして今、あなたの旅行がいつでも楽しめるように計画しましょう。

And now, just plan to enjoy your trip, whenever it comes around.

第6話：海外での食料品の買い物

STORY 6 : FOOD SHOPPING ABROAD

IMPORTANT: The link to download the MP3 is available at the end of this book (page 81).

外国で食べ物を買うことは、喜びであり学ぶことの経験でもあります。そのことはあなたがたくさんの文化の違いを見て、そして理解することを可能にし、そしておそらく、異なる生活様式を理解することをも可能にします。

Shopping for food in a foreign country is a pleasure and a learning experience. It enables you to see and understand so many cultural differences and, perhaps, to understand the different way of life.

寒い国では、そこに住む人々は暖かくするために余分なカロリーを消費する必要があるので、食べ物はかなり重くて、多くは炭水化物です。彼らは自分の胃をいっぱいにし、内側から温める食べ物を選びます。そして調理するのに長い時間がかかるかもしれません。彼らは、必要ならば何時間もオーブンに火をつけ、燃やしたりして自分の食べ物を徹底的に調理します。寒い気候では、これは追加のカロリーの源です。多くの場合、スーパーマーケットには少しつまらないように見える食べ物しかありません。地下や暗闇の中で育ち、太陽にほとんど当たらないので、ほとんど色がありません。それゆえ、それはおいしくなさそう、または味がなさそうに見えることがあります。それは確かに食べたくないように見えるかもしれませんが、それでもおいしいでしょう。

In cold countries, food is often heavy and full of carbohydrates, as the people who live there need to burn extra calories to keep themselves warm. They choose foods that will fill their stomachs and warm them from the inside, and which may take a long time to cook. They are happy to have an oven on, or a fire burning, for hours if necessary, to cook their food thoroughly. It is an additional source of heat in a cold climate. Often, the supermarkets only contain food which looks a little boring. It has little colour as it's grown underground or in the dark, and sees little sun. It can therefore seem unappetising or uninteresting. It certainly looks less tempting to eat, but will still be tasty.

一方、暖かい国では、あまり料理をしたくないという人もいます。彼らは家をさらに暖かくしてしまうために、ストーブや火を使い熱することを望みません。そして彼らは体の中に熱い食べ物を入れたくありません。生のまま食べるのが簡単なので、新鮮な果物や野菜、サラダなどがよく見られます。また、調理しても調理に時間がかからないものもよくあります。

In warmer countries, on the other hand, people often prefer not to cook very much at all. They do not want the heat from an oven or fire to make their home even warmer, and they do not want to put hot food inside their body. They may choose simple food that is best eaten raw, so fresh fruit and vegetables, and salads, are often what is seen, as well as foods that, if cooked, take little time to cook through.

暖かい国の市場やスーパーマーケットでは、色とりどりの果物や野菜があなたの味覚を魅了します。また、幅広い種類のハーブもあります。太陽は手に入る食品に色をもたらします。あなたが以前に見たことも聞いたこともない食べ物がしばしばあるでしょう。これらは様々な魚と並んで見られることが非常に多く、そのうちのいくつかは地元の水域でしか見られません。

In the markets and supermarkets in a warm country, you will see an array of colourful fruit and vegetables to tempt your palette, as well as a big range of herbs. The sun brings colour to the foods available. There will often be foods you have never seen or heard of before. These will very often be seen alongside a variety of fish, some of which are only found in the local waters.

あなたが旅行するとき、地元の食物を食べて楽しんで、そしてあなたが経験している文化を受け入れるように努力をしてください。

When you travel, make an effort to eat and enjoy the local foods and to embrace the culture you are experiencing.

第7話：休暇の忙しい一日(1)

STORY 7 : A BUSY DAY IN THE HOLIDAYS (1)

IMPORTANT: The link to download the MP3 is available at the end of this book (page 81).

「お父さん！お父さん！泳ぎに行ける？」

"Dad! Dad! Can we go swimming?".

「今は寝る時間だ。朝になったら、そのことについて話そう。」

"It's time for bed now. We can talk about it in the morning."

それは学校の休みで、私は教師なので、息子のヘンリーの面倒を見ます。そして犬、チャーリーの世話もです。ヘンリーは8歳で元気いっぱいで、わんぱくです。彼は外に出かけて毎日何かをしたいと思っているのですが、私たちも家でいくつか仕事をする必要があります。

It's the school holidays and, as I am teacher, I look after our son, Henry. And the dog, Charlie. Henry is 8 years old and full of energy, and wants to be busy. He wants to go out and do something every day but we need to do some jobs at home as well.

彼は毎日早く起きて今日も変わりません。私たちが泳ぎに行けるかどうか彼はすぐに聞いてきます。私は彼に取引をしようと言います。

He gets up early every day and today is no different. He asks immediately if we can go swimming. I offer him a deal.

「仕事が終わったら泳ぎに行くことが出来るぞ。仕事を手伝ってくれないか？」

"We can go swimming when we have finished some jobs. Will you help me to do the jobs?"

迷っている様子で、彼は私を見て、自分がしなければならないかもしれないことについて緊張しています。彼は答えないので、私は説明します：

He looks at me, still unsure, nervous about what he might have to do. He doesn't answer so I explain:

「食器洗い機を空にし、食器を洗い、洗濯し、掃除機をかける必要がある。どれをやりたい？」私は彼に聞きます。

"We have to empty the dishwasher, wash up, put the washing on, and hoover. Which do you want to do?", I ask him.

まだ迷っている様子で、彼は私をもう一度見ます。

He looks at me again, still unsure.

最終的に彼は、「代わりに車を洗うのはいい?」と言います。

Eventually he says, "Can I wash the car instead?".

私は彼の提案について慎重に考えます。車は掃除する必要がありますが、私はあまりにも簡単にそれを受け入れたくはありません。私は彼に、やるべきつらい仕事があること、そして彼がごほうびを受けるには自ら勝ち取らなければならないことを理解してほしいのです。

I think carefully about what he is offering. The car does need cleaning but I don't want to give in too easily. I want him to understand that there is hard work to do and he has to earn his treats.

私は彼が前に一度私の車を洗ったことを覚えていますが、私は彼と一緒でした。今回彼は自分ひとりでそれをする必要があります。

I remember that he washed my car once before, but I was with him. This time he needs to do it on his own.

私は少し黙り、キッチンを歩き回りながら考えます。彼は私に何度も「お父さん、お願い、代わりに車を洗ってもいい?」と聞いてきます。

I pause and wander around the kitchen, thinking. He asks me over and over, "Please Dad, can I wash the car instead?".

ある程度考えた後で、私はそれを受け入れ、彼をガレージに連れて行き、バケツ、スポンジ、そして車のシャンプーを見つけ、彼にその仕事を任せます。

After a reasonable pause, I give in. I take him to the garage to find the bucket, sponge and car shampoo, and leave him to it.

ラジオを聞きながら安心して、私は自分の仕事を家の中で続けます。私は15分ごとに彼をチェックします。彼は一生懸命働いていて、自分の仕事に真剣に取り組んでいるようです。

I carry on with my jobs in the house, in peace and listening to the radio, and I check on him every 15 minutes. I see he is working hard and taking his job seriously.

彼は仕事を終え、「お父さん、終わった」と叫び、スポンジをバケツに投げ入れ、そして私は彼の仕事をチェックするために外に出ます。

He finishes and throws the sponge into the bucket with a shout of, "Dad, I've finished," and I go outside to check his work.

私は自分の車がどんなにきれいで輝いているかに驚き、彼がすばらしい車のクリーナーであることを彼に話します。

I am amazed at how clean and shiny my car is and tell him he is an amazing car cleaner.

私たちは家に戻り、水着を入れ、そしてプールに向かいます。

We go back into the house and pack our swimming clothes, and head to the swimming pool.

スイミングの後で、彼は「とっても楽しかった、お父さん。僕は本当にごほうびをもらったと実感したよ!」と言います。

After our swim, he says, "I really enjoyed that, Dad. I really feel as if I earned my treat!".

そして私は彼の意見に同意します。

And I agree with him.

第8話：チョコレートケーキ

STORY 8 : CHOCOLATE CAKE

IMPORTANT: The link to download the MP3 is available at the end of this book (page 81).

ケーキを焼くときは、次の点に注意してください：

When baking cakes, remember the following:

ケーキは温かいうちに食べるほうがいいです。

熱くなった皿に触れると、火傷をする可能性があります。

慎重に材料を量らなければいけません。

新鮮なうちに楽しんでください。

Cakes are better eaten warm.

Hot dishes can burn you if you touch them.

You must measure the ingredients carefully.

It is better to enjoy them while they are fresh.

チョコレートケーキを作るときのいくつかの重事項について考えてみましょう。

Let's think about some important details when making a chocolate cake.

- 材料：
- 小麦粉100グラム
- 砂糖100グラム
- バター100グラム
- 卵2個

チョコレート - 本物のチョコレートまたは粉末

INGREDIENTS:

- 100 grams of flour
- 100 grams of sugar

- 100 grams of butter

- 2 eggs

- Chocolate – real chocolate or powdered

あなたが注意して作り方に従っていけば、おいしくなるでしょう。

If you follow the instructions carefully, it will be delicious.

1. **すべての材料を前もって購入し、まだ新鮮なうちに使用します。**

1. Buy all of the ingredients in advance and use them while they are still fresh.

2. **卵、小麦粉、バター、砂糖などの主成分を慎重に量り、滑らかでクリーミーになるまで混ぜ合わせます。これには5〜10分かかります。バターはすでに柔らかい方が簡単です。**

2. Measure out the main ingredients - eggs, flour, butter and sugar - very carefully and then mix them together until the mixture is smooth and creamy. This may take 5 to 10 minutes. It is easier if the butter is already soft.

3. **混ぜ合わせたものを冷蔵庫で10分間冷やしたら、溶かしたチョコレートを加えます。本物のチョコレートを加える場合は、ゆっくりゆっくりと溶かしてください。チョコレートを過熱しすぎると、塊になってしまい、使うことができないでしょう。溶かしたチョコレートの代わりに粉末チョコレートを加えたい場合、それが最初にふるいにかけられていることを確認し、それからケーキの混ぜ合わせたものにゆっくり加えてください。**

3. Add the melted chocolate when the mixture has cooled in the fridge for 10 minutes. If you add real chocolate, melt it very gently and slowly. If you overheat the chocolate, it will go lumpy and you will not be able to use it. If you prefer to add powdered chocolate instead of melted chocolate, make sure it is sieved first and then add it slowly to the cake mixture.

4. **ケーキが均等に調理されるように、そして、混ぜ合わせたものを入れて調理する準備ができたときにオーブンが十分に温かくなるようにオーブンの電源を入れます。**

4. Turn on the oven so that it is warm enough when you are ready to put the mixture in to cook, and so that the cake is cooked evenly.

5. **混ぜ合わせたものを油を塗った皿(または2皿)に注ぎます。**

5. Pour the mixture into a greased dish (or 2 dishes).

6. **皿の準備ができたら、オーブンに入れます。20分間調理します。**

6. When the dishes are ready, put them in the oven. Cook for 20 minutes.

7. ケーキが出来たら、オーブンから取り出すときに熱くなりますので、手でオーブン皿に触れないでください。耐熱ミトンを使用してください。

7. When the cake is ready, remember not to touch the baking dish with your hands when you take it out of the oven as it will be too hot. Use an oven glove.

8. ケーキを皿から出して冷まします。

8. Turn the cake out of its tin and leave to cool.

9. 冷めたら、スライスに切ってお楽しみください。

9. Once cool, cut a slice and enjoy.

第9話 : スコーンの焼き方

STORY 9 : HOW TO BAKE SCONES

スコーンは伝統的で有名なティータイムのおやつであり、そして作るのがとても簡単です。このスコーンのレシピは、違う味や中身を試したい場合にも簡単に変えることができます。

Scones are a classic English tea-time treat, and are very easy to make. This scone recipe is also easy to change if you want to try a different flavour or filling.

材料:

- ベーキングパウダーなどの膨張剤が入った小麦粉 225g
- 塩一つまみ
- ソフトバター55g
- グラニュー糖 25g
- 牛乳150ml
- 放し飼いの鶏の卵 1つ、表面に塗るための溶き卵(代わりに、少量の牛乳を使うこともできます)

INGREDIENTS:

- 225g of self-raising flour
- a pinch of salt
- 55g of soft butter
- 25g of caster sugar
- 150ml of milk
- 1 free-range egg, beaten, to glaze (although you could, alternatively, use a little milk).

方法:

METHOD:

1. オーブンを200°Cに加熱します。

1. Heat the oven to 200°C.

2. **ベーキングシートに薄くバターを塗るか、またはその上に クッキングペーパーを置きます。**

2. Lightly grease a baking sheet, or put a piece of greaseproof paper on it.

3. **小麦粉と塩を混ぜ、柔らかくしたバターで擦ります。**

3. Mix together the flour and salt, then rub in the softened butter.

4. **砂糖を少しずつかき混ぜ、牛乳を加えて柔らかい生地にします。**

4. Stir in the sugar, a little at a time, and then add the milk to make a soft dough.

5. **ボウルの中で混ぜ合わせた塊を両手でしっかりと混ぜ、次にそれを小麦粉の上に置き、再度軽くこねます。**

5. Work the mixture well with your hands in the mixing bowl, then turn it out onto a floured surface and knead it again lightly.

6. **混ぜ合わせた塊を厚さ約2cmの円形に広げます。丸形/それぞれの形のスコーンを作るために5cmのカッターを使用して、天板の上に置きます。**

6. Pat out the mixture into a round shape roughly 2cm thick. Use a 5cm cutter to make rounds / individual scones, and place them on the baking sheet.

7. **生地の残りの部分をかき混ぜ、手順6を繰り返します。スコーンを作るためにすべての塊を使用するまでこれを続けます。**

7. Pull together what is left of the dough and repeat Step 6. Keep doing this until you have used all of the mixture to make scones.

8. **スコーンの上に溶き卵(または牛乳)を塗ります。天板をオーブンに入れます。**

8. Brush the tops of the scones with the beaten egg (or the milk). Put the baking sheet in the oven.

9. **表面が盛り上がって金色になるまで12〜15分間焼きます。**

9. Bake for between 12 and 15 minutes until well risen and golden on the top.

10. **金網台の上で冷やして、バターとジャム(ストロベリーがよく合います)、またはバターの代わりに凝固した濃厚なクリームを添えて出します。**

10. Cool on a wire rack and serve with butter and a good jam (strawberry works very well), or maybe some clotted cream instead of the butter.

ステップ4でドライフルーツを加えることでレシピを変えることができます。また、ナツメグやシナモンなどのスパイスを加えることもできます。

第9話：スコーンの焼き方　　　　　　　　　　　　　　　　　STORY 9 : HOW TO BAKE SCONES

You can change the recipe by adding dried fruit at Step 4. You can also add some spices such as nutmeg or cinnamon.

砂糖を省略し、粉チーズ100グラムを追加することでチーズ（香ばしい）スコーンを作ることができます。チェダーのような濃いチーズが最も効果的です。

You can make cheese (savoury) scones by leaving out the sugar and adding 100 grams of grated cheese. A strong cheese such as cheddar works best.

召し上がれ！

Enjoy!

第10話：インターネット

STORY 10 : INTERNET

近代技術の出現で、今日の人々は古い世代に比べてより便利で快適な生活を楽しむことができます。

With the advent of modern technology, people today can enjoy more convenient and comfortable lives compared to the older generations.

この情報化時代において、Google、SafariおよびBingのような検索エンジンは、その便利さおよび可能性のために最も広く使用されているコンピュータアプリケーションの一つです。

In this Information Age, search engines such as Google, Safari and Bing are amongst the most widely used computer applications because of their convenience and potential.

基本的なコンピュータースキルだけで、人々は自分の好奇心を満たすと同時に自分の問題に対する答えを簡単に見つけることができます。

With only basic computer skills, people can easily find answers to their problems at the same time as satisfying their curiosity.

多くの学生は学術目的のために検索エンジンを過剰に使用しています。彼らは時々情報のために検索エンジンだけに頼り、本を読んだり、仲間の学生と会話をしたりすることのような他の情報源を探すことをしません。彼らは簡単に自分自身の好奇心を失う可能性があります。

Many students make excessive use of search engines for academic purposes. They sometimes rely solely on search engines for their information and do not explore other sources of information, such as reading books or engaging in conversations with their fellow students. They can easily lose their sense of curiosity.

賢い学生は、公共のオンラインの情報源よりも現実の世界から情報を入手するのにより多くの時間を費やすので、彼らはより面白く個性的で興味深い答えを思い付きます。

Wise students spend more time gathering their information from the real world rather than public, online sources and so come up with more unique, individual, and interesting answers.

コンピューターや技術は人々の生活に欠かせない役割を果たしていますが、それらは彼らのプライバシーにも影響を及ぼします。

Computers and technology do play a vital role in peoples' lives, but they can also affect their privacy.

犯罪者が個人の情報を見ることは容易であり、個人が自分のコンピューターの使用方法について真剣に考えていない場合、これのリスクは高くなります。

It is easy for criminals to see an individual's information and the risk of this is greater if an individual does not think seriously about how they use their computer.

プライバシーの侵害は、このデジタル時代には避けられないように見えるかもしれませんが、そうあるべきではありません。以前は不特定な誰かの銀行の詳細、生年月日、または社会保障番号を、彼ら自身の許可なしに見つけることは、ほとんど不可能でした。しかし、今日、これらの詳細を見つけることがとても簡単なように思われます。

Invasion of privacy may seem inevitable in this digital age, but it should not be. It used to be almost impossible to find out somebody's bank details, date of birth, or social security number, without their permission. But today, these details seem to be so easy to find out.

ソーシャルネットワーキングサイトは、人々が私生活についてオープンになり、犯罪目的または悪意のある目的でそれを使用したい他の人々にとって有用な情報を共有することを助長します。人々は自然に社交的になり、自身の経験を共有したいと思っていますが、テクノロジーの使用によってそれを行うことは彼らに生活の中で問題を引き起こす可能性があります。

Social networking sites encourage people to be open about their private lives and to share information that is useful to others who wish to use it for criminal or malicious purposes. People are naturally sociable and want to share their experiences, but doing so through the use of technology can cause them problems in their lives.

個人は自分の生活を管理することができますし、彼らが自分のコンピューターやインターネットをどのように使用するかはその重要な部分です。

Individuals can take control of their lives and how they use their computer and the Internet is a significant part of this.

第11話：チャネル・トンネル

STORY 11 : CHANNEL TUNNEL

イギリスとヨーロッパの間を車で旅行する場合は、チャネル・トンネルを通過するのが簡単な方法です。

If you want to travel by car between Britain and Europe, travelling through the Channel Tunnel is the easy way to do it.

高速道路でそこに着くことはとても簡単で、案内がしっかりとされています。

Getting there on the motorway is very straightforward and it is well-signposted.

到着すると、それはシンプルなプロセスであり、通常はスムーズに進みます。

Once you arrive, it is a simple process and it usually goes smoothly.

事前予約した場合は、自動料金所を使用できます。予約番号を入力するだけです。あなたの列車が時間通りに運行しているかどうか、そしてそうでなければ何時にあなたが出発できるか分かるでしょう。ユーロトンネルは、事前予約をすることで、予約した電車で確実に旅行できるようになります。忙しい夏の間は十分な時間を取り、事前に予約した出発時刻の45分前に到着することをお勧めします。

If you have pre-booked, you can use an automatic toll booth. You simply enter your booking reference number. You will see if your train is running on time and, if not, what time you can depart. With pre-booking, Eurotunnel does all that it can to ensure you travel on the train you have booked. You are advised to arrive 45 minutes ahead of your pre-booked departure time, although allow plenty of time during the busy summer months.

事前予約していない場合は、到着した時点で支払いが可能です。このオプションを使用すると、スペースがある次の列車で移動します。

If you have not pre-booked, you can pay when you arrive. With this option, you travel on the next train that has a space.

いずれにせよ、あなたの車にぶら下げるための文字コードを与えられるでしょう。ご自分のコードを覚えておいてください！

Either way, you will be given a letter code to hang in your car. Remember your code!

料金所の後、ターミナルに行きます。トイレに行ったり、最後の最後で忘れたもののために店をチェックしたりすると便利です。香水、電気製品、アルコール類、お菓子類、その他たくさんの飲食店があります。

第11話：チャネル・トンネル   STORY 11 : CHANNEL TUNNEL

After the toll booth, you go through to the terminal. It's always useful to visit the toilet and to check the shops for any last-minute items you have forgotten. There is a range of shops offering perfume, electrical items, alcohol and sweets, as well as a number of places to eat.

画面を見て、現在どの列車に乗車しているか、またどの文字コードがその列車に関連しているかを調べます。それはまたあなたの文字が呼ばれる可能性が高いときにあなたに知らせます。これにより、コーヒーを飲む時間があるか、それ以上の時間があるかを知ることができます。

Look at the screens to find out which train is loading currently and which letter code relates to that train. They also let you know when your letter is likely to be called. This helps you to know if you have time for a coffee or something more.

あなたの文字が呼ばれたら、車に戻り、標識に従ってください。列車に乗るために待つ列に参加する前に、入国審査を通過してからセキュリティエリアを通過します。

When your letter is called, return to your car and follow the signs. You will go through passport control and then through a security area, before joining the queue to drive on to the train.

これらの列は厳密に管理されているので、行儀よく行動し、並んで待つ必要があります。

These queues are closely managed and you must behave yourself and wait in line.

列車に乗るように呼ばれたら、慎重に車を運転し、列車はとても小さくて狭いので、ゆっくり列車に入ってください。スタッフがあなたに駐車するように言うまで進みます。

When you are called to board the train, drive carefully and enter the train slowly as it is quite small and narrow inside. Proceed until a member of staff tells you to park.

駐車するときは、セキュリティ情報を注意深く聞かなければいけません。あなた自身の安全と他の旅行者の安全のために、あなたが指示に従うことは非常に重要です。例えば、フラッシュ撮影は許可されていません。

When you park, you must listen carefully to the security information you hear. It is very important that you follow the instructions – for your own safety and that of the other travellers. For example, flash photography is not allowed.

交差点では車で待つように言われます。車の窓は開いたままにしておく必要があります。

You are advised to wait by your car during the crossing, and must leave a car window open.

車両にはセキュリティチェックがあり、そしてエンジンが走行を開始する準備ができているのを聞くことができるでしょう。所要時間はわずか35分です。

There are security checks on the vehicle and then you will hear the engines getting ready to start the journey. The journey itself lasts only 35 minutes, and the time flies by.

何人かのドライバーはその後の旅行を続ける前に眠るためこの時間を使います。他の人はおやつを食べたりゲームをしたりするのに時間を使います。

Some drivers use this time to sleep before continuing their onward journey. Others use the time to eat a snack or to play games.

反対側に到着すると、ドアを開けてあなたが出ていく前に、さらにセキュリティチェックがあります。

When you reach the other side, there are more security checks before they open the doors and you drive away.

チャネル・トンネルを通過するのはとても簡単です。

Travelling through the Channel Tunnel is so easy.

第12話：天気予報

STORY 12 : WEATHER REPORT

これが今後12時間の国の天気予報です。

Here is the country's forecast for the next 12 hours.

本日、国の北部は、寒く湿気があります。大雨が予測され、正午から16時までに最大10cmの降水量が記録されます。また、みぞれとひょうの可能性もあります。この時期の気温は低く、夜になると霜がつくでしょう。運転するときは、特別な注意を払って、そして道路上の氷に用心してください。

In the north of the country today, it is cold and wet. Heavy rain is forecast, with up to 10cm falling between midday and 1600, and there is also a risk of sleet and hail. The temperature is low for the time of year and, as night falls, there is a risk of frost. Take extra care if you are driving, and look out for ice on the roads.

国の西部は午前中はいいですが、特に午後には、雨の危険性が高いです。強風、突風、雷、稲妻を伴う雨が降ったら、嵐に備えてください。傘を持っていき、しかし雷が鳴ったり、稲妻が見えたりする場合は使用しないでください。ペットは室内に入れてください。夕方は乾燥していますがまだ風が強く、気温が上がるため、この時期では通常の気温になります。

The west of the country is looking fair in the morning, but there is still a high risk of rain, especially in the afternoon. Be prepared for some storms if it rains, with strong winds, some gale force, and thunder and lightning. Take an umbrella but remember not to use it if you hear thunder or see lightning, and keep your pets indoors! The evening is dry but still windy, with temperatures rising so that they are normal for the time of year.

国の東部では、特に朝は霧やもやになると予想されます。湿気を感じ、そしてそのため涼しいですが、それは雨のせいではありません。西から来る強い風、強風に注意してください。気温はこの時期では普通で、西の嵐は東に達する前に消えてなくなります。

The east of the country is expected to be foggy or misty, especially in the morning. It feels damp, and therefore cool, but it is not due to rain at all. Beware of strong winds, some gale force, coming from the west. The temperatures are normal for the time of year and the storms in the west will die out before reaching the east.

国の南部では晴れの天気を楽しむことが出来ます。風は弱く暖かい気温で、雨の心配はありません。南部の降雨量はその時期雨量が少なく、一年のうちで気温が高いです。高温のため、外出時には必ず水を持って行くようにしてください。ペットや子供が日焼けや脱水症状を起こす危険がないことを確認してください。

The south of the country is enjoying fine weather. There is a light breeze and warm temperatures, with no risk of rain. Rainfall in the south continues to be low for the time of year, with the temperatures high for the time of year. Because of the high temperatures, make sure you take water with you when you go out. Make sure your pets and children are not at risk of getting sunburn or dehydrated.

明日の天気予報は、晴れで空気が乾燥しているでしょう。

The forecast for tomorrow looks fine and dry.

第13話：休暇の忙しい一日(2)
STORY 13 : A BUSY DAY IN THE HOLIDAYS (2)

ヘンリーと私は、どう仕事が、そして仕事をすることが、ごほうびやお金を得るのに役立つかについて話します。彼は車を掃除してごほうびとして水泳に連れて行ってもらったことを覚えています。

Henry and I talk about how working - and doing jobs - helps you to earn treats or, perhaps, money. He remembers cleaning the car and being taken swimming as his reward.

彼は目覚め - いつものように、元気いっぱい、わんぱくで - そして彼が今日どんな仕事ができるのかを聞きます。

He gets up – full of energy and wanting to be busy, as always – and asks what jobs he can do today.

朝食後、私たちは彼の身体の大きさを考えて、実際にできることについて考えることから始めます。それから今日は何をする必要があるのかについて話します。

After breakfast, we start by thinking about what he can actually do, given his size. Then we talk about what needs to be done today.

私は村の食料品店からいくらか牛乳とパンが必要だと言います。ヘンリーは、芝生は芝刈りをする必要があると言い、私たちは犬を散歩に連れて行かなければいけません。私は、浴室をきれいに掃除する必要があり、そして掃除機をかける必要があることについて言います。

I say we need some milk and bread from the grocery store in the village. Henry says the lawn needs mowing and we must walk the dog. I mention that the bathroom needs a good clean and the house needs to be hoovered.

私たちは、ヘンリーが犬と食料品店に行き、彼を外で結びつけてから、中に入って牛乳とパンを買うことに賛成します。彼は興奮した犬と元気な足取りで出かけます。私はゴム手袋と掃除用品を見つけて、そして浴室を掃除し始めます。これは私の一番嫌いな仕事ですが、ヘンリーにそれをするように言うことはできません。終わったら、棚から掃除機を取り出し、家の中で掃除機をかけます。作業が終わったときにはどこもずっときれいに見えます。

We agree that Henry can walk the dog to the grocery store, tie him up outside, then go in and buy the milk and the bread. He sets off with an excited dog and a spring in his step. I find the rubber gloves and cleaning products, and set to cleaning the bathroom. This is the job I like the least, but I can't ask Henry to do it. When I finish, I then take the hoover from the cupboard and hoover around the house. Everywhere looks and feels much cleaner when I finish.

ヘンリーは、牛乳とパン、そして私たちが後で食べるチョコレートバーを持って犬と一緒に帰ってきます。いいアイデアです！

Henry comes home with the milk and the bread, and the dog, and a bar of chocolate for each of us to have later. Great idea!

私たちは一緒に芝を刈ることにしました。しばらく時間がかかります。私は芝刈り機を押します。そして、ヘンリーは草刈りをします。彼は邪魔にならないようにそれらを角に積み重なった芝生の山の中に入れます。

We decide to mow the lawn together. It takes a while. I push the mower and Henry rakes up the grass cuttings. He puts them in a pile in the corner, out of the way.

もうすぐ昼食の時間であり、私たちはほとんど仕事を終えました。ヘンリーはテーブルを置いて、私はサンドイッチを作ります。私たちは一緒に昼食を食べるために座ります。

It's almost lunch time and we have almost finished our jobs. Henry sets the table and I make us a sandwich. We sit down to eat lunch together.

私たちは午後に何をすべきかを決めようとします。それから二人とも疲れすぎて家の中でリラックスしたいと思っていることで合意し、自分たちの仕事をお互いに褒めあいます。そしてもちろんチョコレートを食べます。

We try to decide what to do in the afternoon and agree that we are both too tired and just want to stay at home and relax, and admire our work. And eat our chocolate, of course.

もう一つの素晴らしいアイデアです！

Another great idea!

第14話：スマートフォン

STORY 14 : SMARTPHONES

スマートフォンがAppleによって発明されて以来、10年以上経ちます。それ以前に携帯電話は十分に一般的でしたが、スマートフォンは私たちがお互いに通信する方法を変えます。

It is just over a decade since the smartphone was invented by Apple. Mobile phones were common enough before then but the smartphone changes how we communicate with each other.

携帯電話での音声通話の数は2017年に初めて減少しました - その事実にもかかわらず、私たちは自分のデバイスに夢中になっています。

The number of voice calls made on mobile phones fell for the first time in 2017 - despite the fact we are hooked on our devices.

現在、全成人の78%がスマートフォンを所有しています。

A total of 78% of all adults now owns a smartphone.

平均して、人々は目覚めているときに12分に1回自分の電話をチェックすると考えられています。

On average, it is believed that people check their phone once every 12 minutes when they're awake.

5人の成人のうち2人が目覚めてから5分以内に自分の電話を見て、3人目は眠る直前に自分の電話をチェックします。

Two in five adults look at their phone within five minutes of waking up, and a third check their phones just before falling asleep.

当然のことながら、高い割合（71%）の人々が電話の電源を切ることは決してなく、78%が公然とそれなしでは生きられないと言っています。

It is understood that a high percentage (71%) of people never turn off their phone and 78% openly say they cannot live without it.

4分の3の人が依然として音声通話を自分たちの電話の重要な機能だと考えており、さらに多く（92%）がWebブラウジングが重要であると考えており、彼らはこれを行うために自分の電話を使います。

Three-quarters of people still regard voice calling as an important function of their phones, more (92%) believe web browsing is crucial, and they choose to use their phone to do this.

携帯電話で電話することは今までで一番簡単ですが、通話の合計数は2017年に1.7％減少したと考えられています。

It is believed that the total number of calls made on mobiles fell by 1.7% in 2017, even though making them is the cheapest it has ever been.

それは必ずしも人々がお互いに話すことが減ったことを意味するわけではなく、彼らはさまざまな方法で話しています。

That does not necessarily mean people are talking to each other less, but they are talking in different ways.

過去10年間で、人々の生活は、スマートフォンの台頭、インターネットへの接続性の向上、そして新しいサービスによって変容してきたということに関して意見が一致しています。私たちはこれまで以上に多くのことをやり遂げることができます。

It is agreed that, over the last decade, people's lives have been transformed by the rise of the smartphone, together with better access to the internet and new services. We can do more on the move than ever before.

人々はスマートフォンが不変の仲間であることに関して意見が一致しています。しかし、彼らがオンラインであるとき自身に負荷を掛け過ぎており、彼らがそうでないときに不満を感じます。

People agree their smartphone is their constant companion, but some are finding themselves overloaded when online, or frustrated when they're not.

家族内では、さまざまな理由で自分のスマートフォンに依存しています。ソーシャルメディアや天気をチェックしたり、買い物リストを保存したりするために使用することができます。他の人はそれをタクシーの予約やEメールの閲覧に使うでしょう。ゲームをしたり、インターネットを検索したり、YouTubeを見たりするためにそれを使用する人もいます。

Within families, different members depend on their smartphones for different reasons. One may use it for checking social media and the weather, and to store shopping lists; another will use it to book taxis and read emails. Others use it to play games, search the internet, and watch YouTube.

そして、いつスマートフォンを使用するのが礼儀をわきまえているのか、またいつそれを見えないところに置いておくかについてのルールを定めている家族もいます。

And some families have rules for when it is polite to use a smartphone and when it should be kept out of sight.

いつ、どこで携帯電話を使用するかについて、あなたは何らかのルールを設けましたか？

Have you set any rules for when and where you use your phone?

第15話：チェスター

STORY 15 : CHESTER

チェスターはイギリスの北西に位置し、ウェールズの国境に非常に近いチェシャー州の首都です。イギリス人の中には、チェスターがイングランドにあるのかウェールズにあるのかわからない人もいますが、確かにイングランドにあります。

Chester is the county town of Cheshire, which is in the north-west of England, very close to the Welsh border. Some British people are uncertain whether Chester is in England or Wales, but it is definitely in England.

州都であるだけでなく、約2000年前から町として存在します。

As well as being the county town, it has been a city for nearly 2,000 years.

チェスターはローマの町で、今日でもたくさんのローマの遺跡を見ることができます。遺跡の中で最も重要なのは、イギリスで最も手つかずの城壁です。容易に壁の周りを歩き回ることができます。これらは元は砦の壁でした。約3キロの長さで、元々の町を囲んでいます。それらはAD 70年とAD 80年の間に建てられました。ローマの円形劇場の遺跡も見られます。その町にいる間にローマ史博物館を是非訪れてください。

Chester is a Roman town and you can still see many Roman sites there today. The most important of the sites is the City Walls which are the most intact city walls in Britain. You can easily walk around the walls; these were the walls of the original fort. They are about 3km long and surround the original town. They were built between 70 AD and 80 AD. You can also see the remains of a Roman amphitheatre. Make sure you visit the Roman History Museum while you're there.

ディー川はチェスターを通り、セーリング、カヌー、ボートツアーの中心地です。長い散歩やピクニックにも最適な場所です。ローマ人はディー川からチェスター・デヴァと名付けました。川はローマ人にとって重要な交易路であり、デヴァは市が必要とする物資を持ち込むための大きな港を持っていました。今となっては 港はもうありません。

The River Dee runs through Chester and it is a centre for sailing, canoeing, and boat trips. It is also a lovely setting for long walks and picnics. The Romans called Chester Deva after the River Dee. The river was a significant trade route for the Romans and Deva had a large harbour to bring in the goods the city needed. The harbour is no longer there.

チェスター城の建設は、大聖堂と同時に11世紀に始まりました。大聖堂はついにAD 1535年に完成しました。

The construction of Chester Castle started in the 11th century AD, at the same time as the cathedral. The cathedral was finally finished in 1535 AD.

チェスターは、おそらく重なり合っているその黒と白の建物で最も有名です。それらは "The Rows" と呼ばれています。今日では、メインショッピングセンターとグランドホテルのザ・グロブナーが入っています。

Chester is perhaps most famous for its black and white buildings which sit on top of each other. They are called 'The Rows'. Today, these contain the main shopping centre and a grand hotel, The Grosvenor.

市の中心部には十字架が付いています。これは、4つのローマの主要道路が交差する地点にあります。

The centre of the city is marked with a Cross, which stands at the point where the 4 main Roman roads meet.

散策するのに膨大な量の歴史を持つ少し変わった場所を訪れたいならば、チェスターについて考えてみてください。

If you want to visit somewhere a little different with a huge amount of history to explore, think of Chester.

きれいな町ですよ。

It's beautiful.

第16話：家族の休日 - パート1

STORY 16 : A FAMILY HOLIDAY – PART 1

ある晩、サラとピーターはワインを飲みながら座っています。ヘンリーはベッドで眠っています。そして、犬のチャーリーは彼らの足元の床で眠っています。

Sarah and Peter sit down with a glass of wine one evening. Henry is asleep in bed and Charlie, the dog, is asleep on the floor at their feet.

「今年は旅行に行きたい？」とピーターはサラに尋ねます。「もし行きたいなら、どこに行きたい？」

"Do you want to go on holiday this year," Peter asks Sarah. "And if you do, where do you want to go?"

サラはしばらくの間考えてこう言います。「ええ、出かけるのはいいわね。新しい仕事は素晴らしいけど、休みを取る準備が出来てるわ。」

Sarah thinks for a few moments and says, "Yes, it will be nice to get away. My new job is great but I am ready for a break."

「それじゃあ、どこに行きましょうか？ 何かアイデアはあるの？」とピーターにもう一度尋ねます。

"Where shall we go then? Any ideas?" asks Peter again.

二人はいくつかの提案をします。ギリシャ、イタリア、ポルトガル。さらに遠くエジプト、チュニジア、トルコ、あるいはアメリカ。それともイギリス？

They both make some suggestions. Greece, Italy, Portugal. Perhaps further afield to Egypt, Tunisia, Turkey, or even the United States. Or maybe England?

それからサラは質問します。「どこに行くべきかを決める前に、休みに何をしたいか決めない？ 私たちがしたいことだけじゃなくて、ヘンリーについてそして彼が何を楽しむかについて考えなければいけないと思う。」

Then Sarah asks, "Can we decide what we want to do on holiday before we decide where to go? I mean, we have to think about Henry and what he will enjoy, not just what we want to do."

ピーターは、賛成して「僕だったら、暖かくて晴れた場所で、ビーチに横になり、泳ぎに行き、ビールを飲み、そして家事をしなくてもいいところがいいな」と言います。それから彼は付け加えます。「でも、ヘンリーはそれを楽しまないだろうな。彼はせわしなく活

発でなくちゃ。やれやれ、僕たち全員が楽しんでプラスになることは何も考えられないよ。」

Peter agrees saying, "Well, if it were up to me, I could just go and lie on a beach somewhere warm and sunny, go swimming, drink beer, and not have to do any house work." The he adds, "But Henry wouldn't enjoy that, would he? He needs to be busy and active. Oh dear, I can't think of anything that we will all enjoy and benefit from."

彼らはそれぞれ黙って座って、ヘンリーを幸せにし、また彼らの生活を容易にするには何をすることができるかを考えます。

They each sit in silence and consider what they can do that will make Henry happy, and also make their lives easy.

やがてピーターは「パリにあるディズニーランド！パリのディズニーランドはどうかな？私たちはいつも行くべきと言っているし、そしてきっとヘンリーはワクワクして素晴らしい時間を過ごすだろう。どう思う？」と大きな声で言いました。

Eventually, Peter shouts out, "Disneyland Paris! What about Disneyland Paris? We always say we should go and I know Henry would be busy and would have a fantastic time. What do you think?"

サラはピーターの笑顔に目を向け、こう言います。「それは完璧だわ。私たちみんなワクワクして楽しむでしょう。そして、ヘンリーはへとへとになるでしょう。でも、それは忘れられない素晴らしい経験になると思うわ。なんて素晴らしい提案なの。計画していきましょう！」

Sarah turns to Peter smiling and says, "I think that would be perfect. We would all be busy and having fun at the same time. Henry will use up a lot of his energy, and it will be a great experience to remember. What a great suggestion. Let's start planning!"

第17話：家族の休日 - パート2
STORY 17 : A FAMILY HOLIDAY – PART 2

決定しました。彼らは休みのためにパリのディズニーランドに行きます。計画を始める時が来ました。

The decision is made. They're going to Disneyland Paris for their holiday. It's time to start planning.

サラとピーターは、オンラインでパリのディズニーランドについて調べ始めます。彼らはそこに行く方法から始めます。

Sarah and Peter go online to start researching Disneyland Paris. They start with how to get there.

彼らにはたくさんの選択肢があるようです。飛行機で行くか、もしくはバスに乗るか、いくつか乗り換えをして電車で移動するか、またはそこへ自分で運転していくこともできます。彼らはドライブで行くアイデアを気に入ったので、それが彼らがすることであると決心します。駐車場はたくさんあるので、それは問題にならないでしょう。

It seems they have a number of options. They can either fly and then take a bus, travel by train with some changes, or drive there themselves. They like the idea of driving so they decide that is what they will do. There is plenty of parking so that won't be a problem.

彼らはそれから宿泊場所をチェックし始め、ディズニーランドにあるホテルのひとつに泊まるなら、それがヘンリーにとってもっと楽しいものになると決心します。彼らがチェックし始めたとき、全てのホテルが全く違うこと、そして非常に大きいことに気づきます。リゾートホテルに泊まると、毎日ディズニーランドまで歩いて行くことができますが、ヘンリーが疲れてしまった時、必要に応じて夜にバスで戻ることができます。

They then start to look at accommodation and decide it will be more fun for Henry if they stay in one of the Disneyland Hotels. When they start looking at them, they realise that they are all very different, and that they're huge. Staying in one of the resort hotels means that they can walk into the park each day but, if necessary, take a bus back in the evening when Henry's legs won't work anymore.

彼らは、さまざまなホテルとさまざまなテーマをチェックしています。彼らはニューポートベイクラブの外観が好きですが、ヘンリーはカウボーイとインディアンが大好きなので、彼はホテルシャイアンが好きだと思います。だから、ホテルシャイアンにします。彼らは日付、費用、そして空室状況を調べます。

They look at the different hotels and their different themes. They like the look of the Newport Bay Club but think that Henry will prefer the Hotel Cheyenne as he loves cowboys and Indians. So, the Hotel Cheyenne it is. They look at dates, costs, and availability.

彼らはそれからどれくらいの間行くのかについて考え始めます。ディズニーランドの両サイドを訪れて楽しむため、まさにそこですべきことについて詳細に調べ始めます。乗り物、ショー、出会うキャラクター達、そして心地よい雰囲気。彼らはディズニーランドでの3泊4日がちょうどいいだろうと決めます。

They then start to think about how long they will go for. With the 2 sides of the park to visit and enjoy, they start to look in detail at what exactly there is to do. Rides, shows, characters to meet, and the atmosphere to soak up. They decide 3 nights with 4 days in the park will be just right.

彼らがちょうど予約をしようとしていた時、チャーリーがいるということに気づき、中断しました。彼らが不在の間、チャーリーはどうしましょうか？犬の世話をするのに十分な犬好きな人を誰も知りませんし、近くの犬の預り所も知りません。

They are about to make a booking when they stop and realise that they have Charlie to think about. What will they do with Charlie while they are away? They don't know anybody who likes dogs enough to look after him for them, and they don't know any kennels nearby.

それから彼らは、パリのディズニーランドには訪れる人々のペットのためのペットセンターがあることに気付きました。完璧な解決策 - チャーリーも一緒に休日を過ごします！

Then they notice that Disneyland Paris has a pet centre for the pets of people visiting the park. Perfect solution – Charlie will have a holiday too!

第18話：家族の休日 - パート3
STORY 18 : A FAMILY HOLIDAY – PART 3

彼らは出発し、そして数時間の旅行の後、高速道路を降りて、ディズニーランドの自分たちのホテルへ向かっています。ヘンリーはとても興奮しています。チャーリーは自分が休暇を取っていることに気付いていませんが、彼もとにかく興奮しています。

They set off and after several hours of travelling, they pull off the autoroute and make their way to their hotel at Disneyland Paris. Henry is so excited! Charlie is not aware that he is having a holiday too, but he is excited anyway.

サラ、ピーター、ヘンリーがホテルシャイアンにチェックインし、チャーリーをしばらく車の中に残しておきます。部屋は素晴らしいですし、ヘンリーは二段ベッドで寝ることに非常に興奮しています。彼は上段か下段の二段ベッドのどちらで寝るか決めることができません。なんて決断なんでしょう！

Sarah, Peter and Henry book in to the Hotel Cheyenne and leave Charlie in the car for a while. The room is amazing and Henry is very excited to be sleeping in a bunk bed. He can't decide whether to sleep on the top or the bottom bunk. What a decision!

数分後、彼らは車に戻ってチャーリーを連れてくることにします。

After a few minutes, they decide to go back to the car and collect Charlie.

「僕たちは今ディズニーランドに向かって、チャーリーをホテルにチェックインさせるかい？」ピーターはヘンリーに提案します。彼らはディズニーランドに行き、訪問者用の駐車場にある動物センターを見つけます。彼らはチャーリーをチェックインさせ、彼がホテルで幸せになることが分かり、ディズニーランドに向かって出発します。

"Shall we head to the park now and check Charlie in to his hotel?" Peter suggests to Henry. They go to the park and find the animal centre which is in the visitor parking area. They check Charlie in and head off towards the park, knowing that he will be happy in his hotel too.

彼らは周りの楽しいディズニーの音楽を聞き、軽やかな足取りで歩きます。彼らは正面玄関に着き、所持品検査を通過します。

They can hear the happy Disney music all around them and walk with a spring in their step. They arrive at the main entrance and go through the bag security checks.

それから彼らは決めなければいけません：メインの場所 - オリジナルディズニーパーク - に行くかどうか、そして従来のディズニーの乗り物に乗るか、それともウォルトディズニースタジオに行くかどうか。なんという選択でしょう！

Then they have to make a decision: whether to go into the main park - the original Disney Park - and do the traditional Disney rides, or whether to go in to Walt Disney Studios. What a choice!

それで、サラはヘンリーに「どこから始める、ヘンリー？」と聞きます。

So, Sarah asks Henry, "Where shall we start, Henry?"

ヘンリーにとって、それは簡単な決断です。「ディズニーパークに行って、キャラクター達を探したい。」

For Henry, it's an easy decision. "Let's go into the Disney Park and look for some characters."

つまり、そこが彼らの行くところです。

So that's where they go.

まっすぐに行き、彼らはメインストリートの始まりの駅の近くでプルートを見つけます。そして彼は微笑んでいる人々に囲まれています。彼らはプルートを追い越して、ミッキーとミニーマウスに向かって歩いていきます。今回、その周りに大勢の人はいません。ヘンリーは、こんにちはと言うために彼らに向かって走ります。

Straightaway, they see Pluto near the railway station at the start of Main Street, and he is surrounded by smiling people. They decide to carry on past him and suddenly see, walking towards them, Mickey and Minnie Mouse. This time, there is no crowd of people and Henry runs towards them to say hello.

ミッキーとミニーは微笑んで手を振り、「ハイタッチ」をヘンリーにします。そしてピーターは3人一緒の写真を撮ります。ヘンリーはチャーリーについて、そして泊まっているホテルについて話します。そして、ミッキーとミニーは笑って興味を持って聞きます。

Mickey and Minnie smile and wave and 'high five' Henry. And Peter takes a photograph of the three of them together. Henry tells them all about Charlie and the hotel they're stating at and Mickey and Minnie listen with interest, smiling.

ヘンリーはとても興奮していて話を止めません。

Henry is so excited and doesn't stop talking.

第19話：家族の休日 - パート4
STORY 19 : A FAMILY HOLIDAY – PART 4

ミッキーとミニーマウスとの珍しい出来事の後、ヘンリーは次に何をしたいのか決めることができないので、ピーターはディズニーランドの地図を取り、それを彼に渡します。

After his adventure with Mickey and Minnie Mouse, Henry can't decide what he wants to do next, so Peter picks up a plan of the park and hands it to him.

「座って、何ができるのかよく見てみましょう。そしたら決めることが出来るわ」とサラは言います。

"Let's sit down and see exactly what there is to do. Then we can decide," says Sarah.

ヘンリーは、とてもお腹が空いていると言い、そして何かする前に食べることができるかどうか聞きます。いいアイデアです。

Henry says he's rather hungry so asks if they can eat before they do anything else. Good idea.

地図を使って、彼らはさまざまなレストランを見ます。ヘンリーはフライドポテトが食べたいと言います。彼はフライドポテトと一緒に何を食べるかは気になりませんが、フライドポテトが欲しいです。彼らはヘンリーがフライドポテトとハンバーガーを食べることができるレストランを選び、サラとピーターはチキンとサラダを食べます。

Using the plan, they look at the different restaurants and Henry declares that he wants chips. He doesn't mind what he has with his chips, but he wants chips. They select a restaurant where Henry can have a burger with chips and Sarah and Peter can have chicken and salad.

食べ物を買い、座ってそして食べ、ディズニーランドの地図を見ます。食べ物はフランスの高級料理ではありませんが、それは全く問題ありません。とても混雑しているので、彼らは乗り物は待つ必要があると知っています。しかし彼らはいくつかの良い乗り物の近くにいることを分かっているので、最初にピーターパンを試すことに決めます。食べ終わったら、彼らはピーターパンの乗り物まで歩いて行き、順番を待ちます。

When they have bought their food, they sit down and eat, and look at the park plan. The food isn't French haute cuisine but it's perfectly fine. They know they will have to queue for the rides as it is so busy, but they realise that they are near to some good rides and so agree to try Peter Pan first. When they finish eating, they walk over to the Peter Pan ride and wait for their turn.

彼らが乗り物に乗って着席すると、ヘンリーはとても興奮しているのですが、ほんの数秒で、彼はサラにもたれかかって眠りに落ち、乗り物の残りの部分を逃します。サラとピーターは、翌日のために十分な体力を確保するために、ホテルに戻って眠る時間だと

決めます。たくさんのウォーキングとワクワクするような長い一日になるでしょう。なので、彼ら全員が良い睡眠を必要としていることに賛成します。

When they join the ride and take their seat, Henry is very excited but within just a few seconds, he falls asleep, leaning against Sarah, and misses the rest of the ride. Sarah and Peter decide it's time to go back to the hotel and get some sleep so that they have enough energy for the next day. It will be a long day with lots of walking and lots of excitement, so they agree that they all need a good night's sleep.

ピーターはヘンリーをバス停まで運び、それから彼らはバスに乗り、ホテルに戻ります。彼らは、ヘンリーが起きないようにベッドに寝かせます。ディズニーランドの地図を見て、明日どこからスタートするかを決めようとしますが、あまりにも疲れているということに同意し、ベッドに行きます。

Peter carries Henry to the bus stop, then they catch the bus back to their hotel. They put Henry to bed without him waking up and sit down themselves to take it all in. They look at the plan of the parks to try to decide where to start tomorrow, but then agree they are too tired, and head to bed themselves.

第20話：家族の休日 - パート5

STORY 20 : A FAMILY HOLIDAY – PART 5

ディズニーランドへの旅行の2日目です。

Day two of the trip to Disneyland.

ヘンリーは非常に疲れているのですが、とても興奮して目が覚めます。彼は早めに朝食をとり、その後ディズニーランドに行きたがっています。朝食には彼はチョコレートシリアルを選び、そしてパンとジャム、オレンジジュースとホットチョコレートを飲みます。

Henry wakes up feeling very tired but very excited. He's keen to go to breakfast early and then into the park. For breakfast he chooses chocolate cereal followed by bread and jam, with orange juice and a hot chocolate to drink.

彼らはまたディズニーランドへ行き、今日はとても暑いと言っています。彼らは再びセキュリティチェックを通過し、そして彼らがそこで見るべき全てを見ることができるようにディズニーランドの中を周る列車に乗ることにします。ヘンリーはとても多くのいろいろな乗り物を見て興奮していて、彼が乗りたい乗り物のリストを作り始めます。

They walk to the park again and comment that it is very hot today. They go through security again, and decide to take the train around the park so that they can see everything there is to see. Henry is excited to see so many different rides and starts to make a list of the rides he wants to go to.

彼らは飲み物を飲むのに一度休むことを決める前に、さらに2つの乗り物に乗ります。サラは気分が悪くなってきたと言います - 頭痛がして吐き気がしています - そして食事も必要です。彼らは列に並ばなければなりません、そしてサラはパニックになり始め、気絶し、そして床に頭を打ちました。ヘンリーは泣き始め、ピーターはサラの横に行き、彼女に話し、確認します。彼は彼女が頭を切っているのを見ます。

They do two more rides before deciding to stop for a drink. Sarah says she is feeling unwell – she has a headache and feels nauseous - and needs something to eat as well. They have to queue and Sarah starts to panic, faints, and hits her head on the floor. Henry starts to cry and Peter gets on to the floor next to Sarah to talk to her and check on her. He sees she has a cut on her head.

3人のディズニーランドのスタッフがサラを助けるために急いで来て、レモネードとコカコーラの2つの飲み物を持ってきて、サラに血糖値を上げるためにそれを飲むように促します。

Three Disneyland staff rush over to help, and bring two drinks, lemonade and Coca-Cola, which they encourage Sarah to drink to help her blood sugar levels.

彼女はレモネードを飲み、コカコーラをヘンリーに渡し、そして彼は泣き止みます。

She drinks the lemonade and gives the Coca-Cola to Henry, and he stops crying.

車椅子を持った男が現れ、サラは診察を受けるために医療センターに連れて行かれます。切り傷から出血が続いているので、彼らはサラがエックス線検査と傷口を縫うために最寄りの病院に行くよう手配し、ピーターとヘンリーは彼女と一緒に行きます。

A man appears with a wheelchair and Sarah is taken to the medical centre to be checked over. The cut keeps bleeding so they arrange for Sarah to go to the nearest hospital for an X-Ray and stitches, and Peter and Henry go with her.

彼女は病院ですぐに医者に見てもらい、なぜ彼女が気を失ったのかをチェックするためのたくさんの検査を受けています。体がとても熱くて非常に疲れている以外に理由が見つかりません。彼女の頭を縫い、それから彼らは休日を続けるためにディズニーランドに戻ります。

She sees a doctor at the hospital very quickly and has lots of tests to check why she fainted. They do not find a reason, other than her being very hot and very tired. They stitch her head and then they all go back to Disneyland to continue their holiday.

ディズニーランドのスタッフはサラについて、とても気にしていて、心配していて、彼らがディズニーランドに戻ったときに無料の食事を提供します。彼らはかなりおなかがすいているので感謝して受け入れます。

The Disneyland staff are very caring and worried about Sarah and offer them a free meal when they are back in the park. They accept gratefully as they are rather hungry.

第21話：家に帰る

STORY 21 : GETTING HOME

ピーター、サラ、そしてヘンリーが荷物をまとめ、ホテルシャイアンをチェックアウトして、チャーリーを引き取りに行きます。彼らは車へと歩いて戻って、パリのディズニーランドでの素晴らしくて慌ただしい旅行の後、家に向かい始めます。

Peter, Sarah and Henry pack their bags, check out of the Hotel Cheyenne, then go and collect Charlie. They walk back to their car and begin to head for home after their fantastic and eventful trip to Disneyland Paris.

彼らはどの道が最短で家に行くのかわかりません。彼らはパリの周りを運転し、正しい帰り道を見つける手助けをするための衛星ナビを使う必要があります。ピーターは自分の住所を座標に設定し、指示を待ちます。

They aren't sure which way to go for the shortest journey home. They need to use satellite navigation (Sat Nav) to help them drive around Paris and to find the right way home. Peter sets the co-ordinates for their address and they wait for their directions.

衛星ナビは、最短ルートの作成に少し時間をかけます。

Sat Nav spends a little time working out the best route.

それから衛星ナビは言います。

Then Sat Nav says:

- ハイライトされたルートに入るとガイドが始まります。
- 幹線道路に着いたら、ロータリーに入り、3番目の出口を出ます。
- 高速道路を10キロ直進します。
- 500m先の次の交差点で右折します。
- 150メートル後、右に進み、高速道路に入ります。
- 右に曲がってください。
- 5キロ直進します。
- ロータリーに入り、2番目の出口を出ます。
- 1キロ先で、左に曲がってください。

- 高速道路に入ります。
- 高速道路を100キロほど進みます。
- 料金所に近づいています。速度を落とし、チケットを用意してください。
- 料金所の後は、左に曲がってください。
- 左に曲がってください。
- 102キロ直進します。
- 800メートル先で、出口を出ます。
- 高速道路を出るときは、左に曲がってください。
- 次の出口で右折し、2キロほど進みます。
- 目的地に到着しました –

- The guidance will start when you join the highlighted route.
- When you reach the main road, enter the roundabout and take the third exit.
- Continue straight on the motorway for 10 kms.
- In 500 metres, at the next junction, keep right.
- After 150 metres, keep right and join the motorway.
- Keep right.
- Continue straight for 5 kms.
- Join the roundabout and take the second exit.
- In 1 km, keep left.
- Join the motorway.
- Stay on the motorway for 100 kms.
- You are approaching a toll booth. Slow down and have your ticket ready.
- After the toll, keep left.
- Keep left.
- Continue straight for 102 kms.

第21話：家に帰る   STORY 21 : GETTING HOME

- In 800 metres, take the exit.

- As you leave the motorway, keep left.

- At the next exit, keep right and follow the road for 2 kms.

- You have reached your destination-

彼らはチャネル・トンネルに近づくと、入る料金所を選びます。

As they approach the Channel Tunnel, they select a toll booth to approach.

サラとピーターは、事前予約して自動料金所を選びました。彼らは早く到着し、トンネルを通るもっと早い列車に乗ることができるのがわかりうれしいです。

Sarah and Peter have pre-booked and select the automated booth. They have arrived early and are pleased to see that they can take an earlier train through the Tunnel.

彼らはターミナルで文字コードが呼ばれるのを待ち、待っている間に、昼食にいくつかサンドイッチを買います。

They wait in the terminal for their letter code to be announced, and buy some sandwiches for lunch while they are waiting.

15分後、彼らの文字コードが呼ばれ、車を運転するために、列車に車を運転するのに戻って歩き、家に帰ります。

After 15 minutes, their letter code is called and they walk back to their car to drive to the train and the return home.

第22話：買い物とランチ(1)

STORY 22 : OUT SHOPPING AND FOR LUNCH (1)

サラはパリのディズニーランドでの彼女の問題の後に気分が良くなっています。

Sarah is feeling better after her problem at Disneyland Paris.

仕事に戻る前に、ランチのために友人 - ナタリー - に会うことを決めます。

Before she goes back to work, she arranges to meet a friend – Natalie - for lunch.

彼女らは金曜日に町で会い、ランチを食べる前に買い物に行きます。

They meet in town on Friday and go shopping before having lunch.

サラは仕事に新しい服が必要だと判断します。スーツ、おしゃれなシャツ、ドレス、そして間違いなく新しい靴です。

Sarah decides she needs some new clothes for work: a suit, a smart shirt, a dress, and definitely some new shoes.

彼女らはまず大きなデパートに行き、女性服売り場でふさわしい服を探し始めます。

They go first into a large department store and start looking for suitable clothes in the ladies' clothes departments.

サラはゆっくりと周りを歩いていますが、彼女が好きなものは何も見つかりません。ナタリーはいくつか提案しますが、それでもサラは興味がありません。突然、彼女は自分が好む青いドレスを見てそれを試着します。彼女はそれが大きすぎると言うので、もっと小さいサイズを探します。彼女はその緑色があるかどうかも聞きます。緑は彼女の好きな色です。緑色は在庫がなく、青色だけあります。

Sarah walks around slowly but sees nothing she likes. Natalie makes some suggestions but still Sarah is not interested. Suddenly, she sees a blue dress that she likes, and tries it on. She says it is too big and she asks for a smaller size. She also asks if it is available in green. Green is her favourite colour. It is not available in green, only in blue.

彼女は小さいサイズを試してみて、それが小さすぎると感じているので、更に探します。

She tries the smaller size and it feels too small so she keeps looking.

彼女は紺色の別のドレスを見てそれを試着します。今回は小さすぎるので、彼女はもっと大きなサイズあるか聞きます。そして、それは在庫があるので、試着します。それは完全にサラに似合っていて、ナタリーはよく似合っていると言うので、サラはそれを買うこ

第22話：買い物とランチ (1) — STORY 22 : OUT SHOPPING AND FOR LUNCH (1)

とにします。ナタリーは前から青いドレスを試着することにしていて、そして、それは完全に彼女に似合っています。なので彼女は自分のためにそれを買うことにします。

She sees another dress in navy blue and tries it on. This time it is too small, so she asks for a larger size, which is available, then tries that on. It fits perfectly and Natalie says it looks great, so Sarah decides to buy it. Natalie decides to try on the blue dress from earlier and it fits her perfectly, so she decides to buy that for herself.

サラとナタリーは、ふさわしいスーツを探すためにさまざまな売り場に行きます。サラは自分が望む色を決めることができません。彼女は賢く見えたいのですが、さまざまなトップスやシャツを着てスーツを着たいと思っています。ナタリーは、グレーは非常に用途が広くあらゆる色に対応すると言って、グレーのスーツを探すことを提案します。

Sarah and Natalie go to a number of different departments to look for a suitable suit. Sarah can't decide what colour she wants. She wants to feel smart but wants to wear the suit with a number of different tops or shirts. Natalie suggests she look for a grey suit, saying grey is very versatile and goes with any colour.

サラはすぐに好きなグレーのスカートを見つけ、それに合うように彼女のサイズのジャケットを探します。店員はそのスカートに合うジャケットはないと言い、そしてサラが好きではあるのですが、それほどで好きではない別のスカートを提案します。

Sarah immediately spots a grey skirt she likes and looks for a jacket in her size to go with it. The shop assistant says they do not have a jacket that goes with that skirt, and suggests a different skirt which Sarah likes, but not as much.

サラはがっかりして、ナタリーに聞きます。「ランチを食べない？　とってもお腹が空いているわ！」

Sarah is disappointed and asks Natalie, "Are you ready for lunch yet? I'm starving!"

ナタリーはランチに行くことを喜んで、どこへ行くべきかについて話し始めます。

Natalie is happy to go for lunch and they start to talk about where to go.

第23話：買い物とランチ(2)
STORY 23 : OUT SHOPPING AND FOR LUNCH (2)

サラとナタリーはどこへランチに行くか話し始めることにします。

Sarah and Natalie agree to go for lunch and start to talk about where to go.

「私はかなりお腹が空いているわ。」とサラは言います。「イタリア料理はどう？ピザ、それともパスタ？」

"I'm rather hungry," says Sarah. "Would you like some Italian food? A pizza or some pasta perhaps?"

ナタリーははっきりしません。「私はイタリア料理が食べたいと思わないわ。どこか中華料理はどう？それは大丈夫？」

Natalie is not sure. "I'm not sure I want Italian food. How about a Chinese meal somewhere? Would that be OK?"

サラはがっかりして、妥協案としてハンバーガーとフライドポテトを提案します。「代わりにハンバーガーを食べたい？」と彼女は聞きます。

Sarah is disappointed and suggests a burger and chips as a compromise. "Would you like to have a burger instead?" she asks.

「うーん。わからない。」とナタリーは言います。「私はフライドポテトはいいけど、ハンバーガーは嫌よ。」

"Mmmm. I'm not sure I do," answers Natalie. "I like the idea of chips but not the burger."

二人ともしばらく黙って考えています。

They both think silently for a while.

「フィッシュ&チップスはどう？」とサラは言います。

"What about fish and chips then?" asks Sarah.

「いいわね！」とナタリーは言います。「完璧！」

"Yes!" says Natalie. "Perfect!"

彼女らはフィッシュ&チップスバーに行き、ランチを注文します。二人とも追加の塩とビネガー、そしてマヨネーズ、それと一緒にパンとバターを頼みます。なんて完璧なランチでしょう！

第23話：買い物とランチ(2)   STORY 23 : OUT SHOPPING AND FOR LUNCH (2)

They go to the fish and chip bar and order their lunch. They both ask for extra salt and vinegar, and mayonnaise, as well as bread and butter to go with it. What a perfect lunch!

彼女らはフィッシュ&チップスと一緒にお茶を飲み、買い物について話します。

They drink tea with their fish and chips and chat about their shopping.

サラは、良いスーツが見つからなかったことにがっかりしていると言います。ナタリーは、店員が勧めたスーツを試着するためにデパートに戻ることを提案しますが、サラはどこか他の場所を見たいと言っています。

Sarah says she's disappointed not to have found the right suit. Natalie suggests she go back to the department store to try on the suit the shop assistant suggested but Sarah says she wants to look somewhere else.

彼らはランチの後に別の店に行くことにします。

They agree to go to a different shop after lunch.

彼女らは一緒に歩き、そしてすぐに、サラは好みのグレーのスーツを見つけます。彼女はそれを試着することを尋ねます。

They walk in together and, immediately, Sarah sees a grey suit that she likes. She asks to try it on.

店員はサラのサイズのスーツを見つけ、サラはそれを試着します。彼女が試着室から出てくると、ナタリーは「わあ！それはあなたにぴったりで素敵よ！」と言います。

The shop assistant finds the suit in Sarah's size and Sarah tries it on. She walks out of the changing room and Natalie says, "Wow!", followed by, "That fits you perfectly and looks fantastic!".

サラはほっとして笑っています。彼女はそれを買おうと決心し、クレジットカードを財布から取り出して支払います。彼女は店員に「それはいくらですか？」と尋ねます。彼女はそのスーツがセールで、たった150ユーロであることを知って、とても驚いて喜んでいます。

Sarah is so relieved and smiles. She decides to buy it and takes her credit card from her purse to pay. She asks the assistant, "How much is that?". She is surprised and pleased to learn the suit is in the sale and only costs €150.

なんてお買い得なの！

What a bargain!

第24話：買い物とランチ(3)

STORY 24 : OUT SHOPPING AND FOR LUNCH (3)

サラは今、彼女の買い物について気分が良くなっていて、欲しいシャツと靴について考え始めています。

Sarah is feeling good about her shopping trip now and starts to think about her shirt and the shoes she wants.

サラとナタリーはデパートに戻って女性用のシャツを探し、いくつかの売り場で大きな選択の機会があることが分かります。

Sarah and Natalie go back to the department store to look for ladies' shirts and find there is a huge choice in a number of departments.

サラは、どれだけの選択があるかに驚いていて、彼女はグレーのスーツを着るために2枚のシャツを買うことにします。

Sarah is amazed how many there are to choose from and decides she will buy two shirts to go with her grey suit.

まず、彼女は白いシャツを探します。シンプルでクラシックなものです。彼女は3つ見つけて、試着します。1つは大きすぎ、1つは小さすぎ、そして最後の1つは袖が長すぎる以外はぴったりです。彼女は更に探します。

First, she looks for a white shirt. Simple and classic. She finds three and tries them on. One is too big, one is too small, and one fits well except the sleeves are too long. She continues looking.

彼女は更に2つ見つけますが、そのうちの1つはサイズを見つけることができません。彼女は自分のサイズがあるかどうか店員に尋ね、店員はそれを見つけるために離れていきます。彼女は喜んで戻ってきます。そしてサラは2枚のシャツを試着します。

She finds two more but can't find her size in one of them. She asks the shop assistant if they have her size and she goes away to find it. She comes back happy, and Sarah tries on the two shirts.

今回は、両方とも完璧であり、彼女は決断をするのが難しいです。あら！サラはナタリーに両方のシャツを見せます。そして、すぐに、ナタリーは彼女にどちらを買うべきか言います。

This time, they are both perfect and she has a difficult decision to make. Oh dear! Sarah shows both shirts to Natalie and, straightaway, Natalie tells her which one to buy.

第24話：買い物とランチ(3)　　　　　　　　　　　　　　　　　　　　　　STORY 24 : OUT SHOPPING AND FOR LUNCH (3)

サラは同意してから、別の色のシャツを探します。彼女はピンク色の同じシャツを見つけて喜んでいます。だから、サラは同じスタイルの2枚のシャツを購入します。1枚は白、もう1枚はピンクです。

Sarah agrees and then looks for another shirt in a different colour. She finds the same shirt in pink and she is delighted. So, Sarah buys 2 shirts the same style, one in white and one in pink.

ナタリーは、彼女に靴も探していると彼女に思い出させ、そして、靴売り場に向かいます。

Natalie reminds her that they are also looking for shoes, and they head for the shoe department.

サラはいくつかおしゃれな黒い靴を探すことを決めます。そして、ナタリーは仕事のためにいくつか紺色の靴を欲しいと付け加えます。

Sarah decides to look for some smart black shoes, and Natalie adds that she wants some navy blue shoes for work.

彼女らは二人ともすぐに紺と黒の両方のいくつかのおしゃれな革靴を見つけます。店員にサイズを尋ねます - サラは39で、ナタリーは37です - そして驚いたことに、店は両方の色で両方のサイズがあります。

They both immediately see some smart leather shoes which seem to be available in both navy blue and black. They ask the assistant for their size – Sarah is a 39 and Natalie is a 37 – and to their surprise, the shop has both sizes in both colours.

彼女らはそれらを試着し、その売り場をしばらく歩き回り、そして買うことにします。

They try them on, walk around the department for a short while, then decide to buy them.

サラはとても充実した買い物の日を過ごし、たくさんのお金を使い、家に帰ります。まあ、しかたがないですね…

Sarah goes home having had a very successful shopping day and having spent a great deal of money. Oh well…

第25話：休暇の終わり（1）

STORY 25 : END OF THE HOLIDAYS (1)

それは休暇の最後の週で、ピーターはヘンリーに何をしたいのか聞きます。

It is the last week of the holidays and Peter asks Henry what he would like to do.

毎週、ヘンリーは地元のスポーツセンターのサマーキャンプに行きます。そして、彼はそこで友達と会うので、いつも通りそれをしたいと言います。

Every week, Henry goes to the summer camp in the local sports centre and he says he still wants to do that as usual as he meets his friends there.

ピーターはそれについて満足して、賛成します。それから彼は他の日のいくつか提案をします。

Peter is pleased about that and agrees. Then he makes some suggestions for the other days.

「えっと、分かりきっていることだけど、いつか君に新しい制服を買う必要があるな。」とピーターは言います。

"Well, we need to buy you some new school uniform one day, I know that," says Peter.

ヘンリーは、「僕たちいつかお菓子を焼くことできる、お父さん？ずっと長い間何も焼いてないよ。」と聞きます。

Henry asks, "Can we do some baking one day, Dad? We haven't done baking for ages."

「そうだな、焼いていないな。」とピーターは同意します。「チョコレートケーキとスコーンを作れるだろう。でも、家事をまたする必要があるよ。家を出て、庭をきれいに整えないといけない。」

"You're right, we haven't," agrees Peter. "We could make a chocolate cake and perhaps some scones? But we need to do some housework again and leave the house, and garden, neat and tidy."

ヘンリーは、これを手伝うことを知っていて、そして最後にごほうびをもらえればいいと思っています。しかし、彼はまた、毎週お小遣いがあるので、もらえないかもしれないことを知っています。

Henry knows he will help with this and hopes he will get a treat at the end. But he also knows he may not because he has pocket money every week.

「チャーリーを散歩に連れて行くことから始めよう。」ピーターはヘンリーに提案します。

第25話：休暇の終わり(1) — STORY 25 : END OF THE HOLIDAYS (1)

"Let's start by taking Charlie for a walk, shall we?" Peter suggests to Henry.

「その時公園に行ける?お父さん?」とヘンリーは言います。ヘンリーは、ボールを公園に持っていってチャーリーにそれを投げて、追いかけて取って戻ってくるのが大好きです。

"Can we go to the park then, Dad?" asks Henry. Henry loves taking a ball to the park and throwing it for Charlie to run after and bring back.

ヘンリーは2階に上がり、散歩のためそして公園で遊ぶために着るトレーナー、そしてピーターはチャーリーのリードを取ります。チャーリーは、彼らが散歩に出かけようとしていることがすぐに分かり、とても興奮しています。

Henry goes upstairs to get his trainers to wear for the walk and to play in the park, and Peter picks up Charlie's lead. Charlie knows straightaway that they're going for a walk and is vey excited.

家を出る途中で、彼らはテニスボールを持っていきます。

On the way out of the house, they pick up a tennis ball.

公園までは15分かかります。彼らがそこに着くと、走り回って遊ぶためのたくさんのスペースがあるので、彼らは自分たちが公園でたった二人であると思います。ヘンリーとチャーリーはとても興奮していて、投げたり、追いかけたり、捕まえたり、取ったり、1時間以上楽しく遊んでいます。

It takes fifteen minutes to get to the park. When they get there, they find they are the only people in the park so they have lots of space to run around and play. Henry and Charlie are both very excited and play happily for more than an hour, throwing, chasing, catching, fetching.

二人とも疲れきっているのでヘンリーはブランコに座り、チャーリーは近くの地面に横になっています。彼らは歩いて戻るのに待っています。

They are both exhausted so Henry sits on a swing and Charlie lies on the ground nearby. They wait a few minutes before they walk back.

彼らが家に歩いていると、ヘンリーは言います。「お父さん、僕のトレーナーは今小さすぎると思う。明日新しい制服のために買い物に行って、トレーナーも買える?」

As they are walking home, Henry says, "Dad, I think my trainers are too small now. Can we go shopping for my new school uniform tomorrow and buy some trainers as well?"

「ああ、出来るよ。いい考えだ。」とピーターは言います。

"Yes, we can. Good idea," says Peter.

第26話：休暇の終わり(2)

STORY 26 : END OF THE HOLIDAYS (2)

それは休日の最後の週です。ピーターとヘンリーにはするべきことのリストがあります。

It is the last week of the holidays. Peter and Henry have a list of things to do.

今日は新しい制服、特に新しいトレーナーを買う日です。

Today is the day for buying new school uniform and, in particular, new trainers.

ピーターは学校の制服のリストを見つけて、ヘンリーと一緒に調べていきます。ピーターがそれと言い、ヘンリーは去年の制服を見つけて、それがまだ着れるかどうか見るためにそれを試着してみます。もし着れなければ、制服を買い物のリストに含みます。もし着れるなら、良いですね、買うものが一つ少なくなります。

Peter finds the school uniform list and starts to go through it with Henry. Peter says the item, and Henry finds the uniform from last year and tries it on to see if it still fits. If it doesn't, it goes on the shopping list. If it does, good, one less thing to buy.

「新しいトレーナーをリストのトップに置こう。僕たちはそれがとても小さいことを知っているから。」とピーターは言います。そして、彼らはそのリストを始めます。

Peter says, "Let's put new trainers at the top of the list. We know they're too small." And they start the list.

買い物リスト：

- トレーナー

SHOPPING LIST:

- Trainers

ヘンリーはショートパンツとズボンを試着して、ショートパンツは合うことがわかりましたが、ズボンは今は短すぎます。

Henry tries on his shorts and trousers and finds the shorts fit, but the trousers are too short now.

- トレーナー
- 濃いグレーのズボン2着

第26話：休暇の終わり(2)　　　　　STORY 26 : END OF THE HOLIDAYS (2)

- Trainers
- 2 pairs of dark grey trousers

それから彼らはポロシャツを試着します。それも今は短すぎます。そして白ではなくて灰色に見えます。それでピーターはそれらもリストに加えます。

Then they try on the polo shirts. They are also too short now, and they look grey rather than white, so Peter adds those to the list as well.

- トレーナー
- 濃いグレーのズボン2着
- 白いポロシャツ5枚
- Trainers
- 2 pairs of dark grey trousers
- 5 white polo shirts

「ヘンリー、スウェットシャツはどこにある？」とピーターは聞きます。

"Where is your sweatshirt, Henry?" asks Peter.

僕は学期の終わりに見つけることができなかった、お父さん。絶対に新しいのが必要だよ。」

"I couldn't find it at the end of term, Dad. I definitely need a new one."

- トレーナー
- 濃いグレーのズボン2着
- 白いポロシャツ5枚
- 赤いスウェットシャツ
- Trainers
- 2 pairs of dark grey trousers
- 5 white polo shirts
- Red sweatshirt

67

トレーナーだけじゃなくて、体育用の服についてはどうだ？体育用の新しいショートパンツが必要かい？」ピーターはヘンリーに聞きます。

"As well as trainers, what about your PE kit? Do you need any new shorts for PE?" Peter asks Henry.

履いてみるよ。」とヘンリーは答えます。彼はそれらがまだ合うことが分かりましたが、彼は新しい体育用の靴下を必要としています。

"I'll try them on," replies Henry. He finds that they still fit, but he needs new PE socks.

- トレーナー
- 濃いグレーのズボン2着
- 白いポロシャツ5枚
- 赤いスウェットシャツ
- 白い体育用靴下

- Trainers
- 2 pairs of dark grey trousers
- 5 white polo shirts
- Red sweatshirt
- White PE socks

僕は新しいグレーの靴下も必要だと思うよ、ヘンリー。それもリストに入れよう。」とピーターは提案します。

"I think you need new grey socks as well, Henry, so let's put those on the list as well," Peter suggests.

- トレーナー
- 濃いグレーのズボン2着
- 白いポロシャツ5枚
- 赤いスウェットシャツ
- 白い体育用靴下
- グレーの靴下5足

- Trainers
- 2 pairs of dark grey trousers
- 5 white polo shirts
- Red sweatshirt
- White PE socks
- 5 pairs of grey socks

そして最後に、彼らはヘンリーのスクールシューズについて考えます。ヘンリーはそれを試着して、そして彼のトレーナーのように、今は小さすぎるので、彼らはまた買い物リストにそれを含む必要があります。

And finally, they think about Henry's school shoes. Henry tries them on and, like his trainers, they are now too small, so they also need to go on the shopping list.

- **トレーナー**
- **濃いグレーのズボン2着**
- **白いポロシャツ5枚**
- **赤いスウェットシャツ**
- **白い体育用靴下**
- **グレーの靴下5足**
- **黒いスクールシューズ**

Peter suggests.

- Trainers
- 2 pairs of dark grey trousers
- 5 white polo shirts
- Red sweatshirt
- White PE socks
- 5 pairs of grey socks
- Black school shoes

ピーターとヘンリーは二人ともそのリストを見て、彼らの目の前に忙しい買い物の日があるということがわかりました。

Peter and Henry both look at the list and agree they have a busy day of shopping ahead of them.

第27話：休暇の終わり (3)

STORY 27 : END OF THE HOLIDAYS (3)

制服の買い物リストを持ち、ピーターとヘンリーは町に行くために車に乗り込みます。

With the school uniform shopping list in hand, Peter and Henry get into the car to drive to town.

彼らが町に着くとき、最初にいくつかトレーナーを買うためにスポーツ店に行きます。ヘンリーは4つの違うトレーナーを試着します。1つはすべて白、そして青と白、赤と黒、最後に白と緑です。ピーターは青と白のトレーナーが一番いいと思いますが、ヘンリーは赤と黒のトレーナーが欲しいです。それは彼に大好きなサッカーチームを連想させるからです。それは他のものより高いですが、ピーターは赤と黒のセーターを買うことに賛成します。

When they arrive, they go first to a sports shop to buy some trainers. Henry tries on 4 different pairs – one all white pair, one pair that is blue and white, one pair that is red and black, and finally a white and green pair. Peter thinks the blue and white look best but Henry wants the red and black, because they remind him of his favourite football team. They cost more, but Peter agrees to the red and black pair.

彼らがスポーツショップにいる間、ヘンリーの白い体育用靴下を買います。

While they are in the sports shop, they buy Henry's white PE socks.

それから彼らは有名なデパートに行き、靴を含んだ他の5つの品物を探します。

They then go to a well-known department store to look for the other five items, including the shoes.

彼らは白いポロシャツをすぐに見つけて、ヘンリーが必要な5着のシャツを買い物かごに入れます。ポロシャツの近くには、違った色のスウェットシャツがあります。ネイビーブルー、緑、紫、黄色、そしてありがたいことに赤色のものも。なので、ヘンリーのサイズの赤いスウェットシャツを買い物かごに入れます。

They find the white polo shirts straightaway and are able to put the five shirts Henry needs into the shopping basket. Near to the polo shirts are the sweatshirts in different colours: navy blue, green, purple, yellow and, thankfully, red. So, a red sweatshirt in Henry's size goes into the shopping basket.

グレーの靴下は見つけるのがとても簡単です - 良いサイズのものがたくさんあります。5組の靴下を買い物かごに入れます。

The grey socks are just as easy to find – there are plenty in the right size. Five pairs go into the shopping basket.

ズボンもたくさん選ぶものがあるとピーターはそう考えます。彼は棚のほぼすべてのズボンを見て、ヘンリーに合ったサイズを1つだけ見つけます。ピーターはそれをかごに入れて店員を見つけようとします。しかし、その後ピーターは、最初の数週間はヘンリーがショートパンツを履いて学校に行くので心配しないことにします。彼らはもう一着をオンラインで注文して、それが届くのを待つことができます。

There are plenty of trousers to choose from as well – or so Peter thinks. He looks at nearly every pair on the racks and only finds one pair that are the right size for Henry. Peter puts them in the basket and tries to find an assistant. But then Peter decides not to worry as Henry will wear shorts for the first few weeks back at school, and they can order a pair online and wait for them to arrive.

彼らはレジまで行き、かごの中の商品の代金を支払います。

They go to the till and pay for the items in the basket.

そして今度は靴です。彼らは靴売り場に行き、そこにはたくさんの靴があり選択肢はたくさんあります。ひも付き、ベルクロストラップ付きのものもあります。ピーターはひも付きの靴がいいと決めます。そして、ヘンリーは彼が本当に快適だと思う靴を試着します。それはまたかっこよく見えます。なので、ピーターは靴の代金も支払います。

And now the shoes. They go to the shoe department where there are many pairs to choose from. Some with laces, some with Velcro straps. Peter decides that laced shoes are better and Henry tries on a pair that he says are really comfortable. They look smart as well. So, Peter pays for the shoes as well.

持ち運ぶものがたくさんあるので、ピーターは帰宅する前に何か飲むことを提案します。買い物でお腹がすいたので、ヘンリーは何か食べるものがあるか聞きます。

With lots of bags to carry, Peter suggests they go for a drink before going home. Henry asks if he can have something to eat as shopping makes him hungry.

ピーターはコーヒーとケーキ、そして、ヘンリーはコカコーラとケーキです。

Coffee and cake for Peter, Coca-Cola and cake for Henry.

第28話：休暇の終わり(4)
STORY 28 : END OF THE HOLIDAYS (4)

今日は、地元のスポーツセンターのサマーキャンプでのヘンリーの最後の日です。

Today is Henry's last day at the Summer Camp in the local sports centre.

彼は起きると、水着とタオルをかばんに入れて、新しいトレーナーを取り出します。

When he gets up, he packs his bag with his swimming costume and towel, and gets out his new trainers.

彼は自分のサッカー道具と新しいトレーナーを身に着けて朝食のために下に行きます。

He puts on his football kit and new trainers and goes downstairs for breakfast.

ピーターはすでに下で昼食のためのヘンリーのサンドイッチを作っています。そして、彼らはヘンリーが今日サマーキャンプで何をするかについて話します。

Peter is downstairs already making Henry's sandwich for lunch, and they talk about what Henry might do today at the summer camp.

「えっと、僕たちはいつもサッカーをするよ。それが一番いいところなんだ。6つのチームと何人かの控えの選手のために十分な人数がいるよ。そして僕たちは日中はトーナメントをするんだ。試合の合間には、水泳やバドミントンをすることができるよ。」とヘンリーは説明します。

"Well, we always play football. That's the best part. There are enough people for six teams and a few substitutes, and we play a tournament during the day. In between games, we can go swimming, or play badminton," Henry explains.

「他にもやることがあるよ。僕たちは選べるんだ。」と、ヘンリーは続けます。

"There are other things to do as well, we choose," Henry adds.

考えて、彼は言いました。「キャンプでの最後の日だから、僕は今日いくつか違ったアクティビティをやってみようと思ってるんだ。」

Thoughtfully, he says, "I think that I will try some different activities today as well, as it is my last day at camp."

「アーチェリーが面白そう。」とヘンリーは言います。「お父さん、どう思う？」

"I like the idea of archery," Henry says. "What do you think, Dad?"

「いいじゃないか。やってみなさい。楽しいと思うぞ。他にどんなアクティビティがあるんだ？」ピーターは聞きます。

"Great. Have a go. It sounds like fun. And what other activities are there to do?" Peter asks.

ヘンリーは答えます。「えっと、プールにはカヌーがあるよ。でも、僕はそれをしたいとは思わない。トランポリンやバスケットボールもあると思う。」

Henry replies, "Well, there's canoeing in the swimming pool. I don't think I want to do that though. There's also trampolining, and basketball, I think."

「もしやりたいなら、全部のアクティビティをすることができるかい？」ピーターはヘンリーに聞きます。

"Can you do all of the activities if you want to?" Peter asks Henry.

「うん。」ヘンリーは答えました。「サッカーの試合の合間にそれをしなきゃいけない！」

"Yes," Henry answers, "You just have to do them between the football matches!"

彼らはヘンリーのお弁当を彼のリュックに入れました。ヘンリーは朝食を終え、そして彼らは出かけます。

They put Henry's packed lunch into his rucksack. Henry finishes his breakfast, and they leave.

チャーリーは一日のことを考えて一人ぼっちで悲しそうです。

Charlie looks sad at the thought of a day on his own.

ピーターはスポーツセンターまで車で行き、ヘンリーを登録デスクまで連れて行きます。たくさんのスタッフ、そしてヘンリーと同じような元気な子供達がたくさんいます。彼らは幸せいっぱいで、お互い会うことに興奮しているようです。そしてピーターは、ヘンリーが素晴らしい一日を過ごすことを知っています。

Peter drives to the sports centre, parks, and takes Henry up to the registration desk. There are lots of staff there, as well as lots of energetic children, just like Henry. They look happy and excited to see each other and Peter knows that Henry is going to have a great day.

そしてピーターもそうです！

And so is Peter!

第29話：休暇の終わり(5)

STORY 29 : END OF THE HOLIDAYS (5)

ヘンリーはサマーキャンプにいます。そして今日は休暇の最後の日です。ピーターは来週教師として働くために戻る前にやりたいことを何でもすることができます。

Henry is at summer camp and today is the last day of the holidays when Peter can do whatever he wants to do before he goes back to work as a teacher next week.

ピーターは長い散歩にチャーリーを連れて行きます。彼らは公園に行き、そして野原を通って行き、8キロメートル歩いて家に着きます。チャーリーは長い眠りのために横になります。

Peter takes Charlie for a long walk. They go to the park and then walk through the fields and arrive home after eight kilometres. Charlie lies down for a long sleep.

ピーターは早めの昼食を準備するために台所に入り、午後の間に彼が本当にやりたいことについて考えるために立ち止まります。

Peter goes into the kitchen to prepare an early lunch and stops to think about what he really wants to do during the afternoon.

彼の選択肢は何ですか?

What are his options?

彼は家でテレビを見ることができます。いいえ、彼はしたいなら、いつでもすることができます。

He can stay at home and watch TV. No, he can do that whenever he wants to.

彼は来週のために買い物に行くことができます。いいえ、彼はいつでも好きなときにオンラインで食べ物を買うことが出来ます。

He can go shopping to buy food for next week. No, he can shop online for food whenever he wants to.

彼はゴルフに出かけることができます。いいえ、彼はむしろそれをするために誰か人がいたほうがいいと思います。一人でするのは好きではありません。

He can go and play a round of golf. No, he would rather have company to do that, he doesn't like playing on his own.

彼は泳ぎに行くことが出来ます。いいえ、彼はまだスポーツセンターに戻りたくありません。

He can go for a swim. No, he doesn't want to go back to the sports centre yet.

彼は芝を刈ること、家を掃除すること、車を洗うこと、そして浴室を掃除することができます。いいえ、彼は明日ヘンリーの助けを借りてそれを行います。それはもっと楽しくなるでしょう。

He can mow the lawn, clean the house, wash the car, and clean the bathrooms. No, he will do that tomorrow with Henry's help. That will be more fun.

彼は新しい仕事用の服を買いに行くことができます。

He can go shopping for some new work clothes.

実際、それは悪い考えではありません。

Actually, that isn't a bad idea.

それから彼は別の考えがあります。彼はサラに電話します。

Then he has another idea. He phones Sarah.

もう昼食を食べたかい?」彼は彼女が電話にでると尋ねます。

"Have you had lunch yet?" he asks her as she answers the phone.

まだよ。私は大体30分後に昼食を食べるわ。」彼女は答えます。

"Not yet. I take my lunch in about half an hour," she replies.

いいね。じゃあ一緒に昼食を食べよう。」とピーターは彼女に言います。「僕は新しい服を買うために町に行く。僕の休暇はもうすぐ終わるから、一緒に静かな昼食を取ることが出来るよ。」

"Fantastic. Let's have lunch together then," Peter says to her. "I'm coming to town to buy some new clothes. We can have a quiet lunch together as my holiday is nearly over."

それは素敵ね。」サラはきっぱりと答えます。「ハイストリートの角にあるイタリアンレストランで会いましょう。私はそれをとても楽しみにしているわ!」

"That would be lovely," Sarah replies, positively. "I will meet you at the Italian restaurant on the corner of the High Street. I am really looking forward to it!"

ピーターはとても喜び、着替えるために2階に走って行きます。

Peter is very pleased and runs upstairs to get changed.

第30話：休暇の終わり(6)

STORY 30 : END OF THE HOLIDAYS (6)

ピーターとヘンリーは、休暇の最終日に一緒に朝食を食べています。サラは早く仕事に行きました。

Peter and Henry are having breakfast together on the last day of the holidays. Sarah has gone to work early.

「ヘンリー、来週学校に戻るとき、私たちは家を清潔できれいにしておくために、すべての家事をする必要があるんだ。」とピーターは言います。

"Henry, today, we need to do all the household jobs so that we leave the house clean and tidy when we go back to school next week," says Peter.

ヘンリーは微笑んで言います。「知ってるよ、お父さん。今日は大変な仕事をする必要があるね。でも、後でお菓子を焼くことはできる？」

Henry smiles and says, "I know, Dad. I know we have to do some hard work today. Can we do some baking afterwards though?"

すべての仕事をし終えたとき、ピーターは午後お菓子を作ることに賛成します。

Peter agrees to a baking afternoon when they have finished doing all their jobs.

ヘンリーは再び車を掃除することを提案します- 彼はそれを楽しみ、そして前回上手にやりました。

Henry offers to clean the car again – he enjoyed that and did it well last time.

まずピーターは、自分の寝室がきれいになっていること、スクールバッグに持ち物が入っていること、そして制服の準備ができていることを確認する必要があることを彼に言います。

Peter tells him that first, he has to make sure that his bedroom is tidy, his school bag is packed, and his uniform is ready.

ヘンリーは寝室を片付けなければならないことに不満で、ゆっくりと2階に上がります。

Henry isn't happy at having to tidy his bedroom, and goes upstairs slowly.

ピーターは食洗器に皿を入れ、台所をきれいにし、そして台所の床をモップにかけます。今、キッチンはほとんど終わっています。

Peter puts the dishes in the dishwasher, cleans the kitchen, then mops the kitchen floor. Now, the kitchen is more or less done.

ピーターはそれから掃除を始めるために2階の浴室に行きます。彼は浴室を掃除するのが嫌いです。

Peter then walks upstairs to the bathrooms to start cleaning there. He doesn't like cleaning the bathrooms.

それをやり終えるとき、洗濯機に洗濯物を入れることを思い出します。それから彼はベッドシーツを変えます。

When he finishes that, he remembers to put some washing in the washing machine. Then he changes the beds.

ピーターはヘンリーに芝刈りをするために外に出ていると言います。彼はヘンリーが寝室にいるのを見つけ、寝室はきれいになっているので、今車を掃除できると言います。

Peter tells Henry that he's going outside to mow the lawn. He finds him in his bedroom and tells him that his bedroom is looking tidy so he can go and clean the car now.

ピーターとヘンリーは一緒に下に行きます。ピーターは芝生を刈り、ヘンリーは車を掃除します。

Peter and Henry go downstairs together. Peter mows the lawn and Henry cleans the car.

ヘンリーは再びとても良い仕事をしています。そして彼が終わったとき車はとても輝いて見えます。

Again, Henry does a very good job and the car is very shiny when he finishes.

ピーターが終わったとき庭園まもたきれいに見えます。

The garden looks good when Peter finishes, as well.

彼らは今昼食の時間だと気づいたので、庭で一緒に座ってサンドイッチを食べます。

They realise it's time for lunch now so they sit down together in the garden and eat a sandwich.

彼らは今朝したことを楽しく振り返り、午後にお菓子を焼くことに賛成します。

They reflect happily on what they have done this morning, and agree that they are going to do some baking in the afternoon.

「どっちを先に作る？チョコレートケーキ？それともスコーン？」ピーターは、ヘンリーに聞きます。

"Which shall we make first? The chocolate cake or the scones?" Peter asks Henry an Henry.

ヘンリーはちょっと考えてこう言います。「お母さんはチョコレートケーキが大好きなので、まずスコーンを作ろう。お母さんが家に帰るとき、ケーキは温かいから、彼女はそれを気に入るはずだよ！」

Henry thinks for a moment and says, "Mum loves chocolate cake so let's make the scones first. The cake will be warmer when Mum gets home and she will love it!".

結論

CONCLUSION

You have just completed the 30 short stories in this book. Congratulations!

We hope that the collection of stories you have read will encourage you to continue learning Japanese. Reading can be one of the best---and most enjoyable--activities you could do to develop your language skills. Hopefully, you were able to experience that with this book.

If fully consumed as we have intended, these Japanese short stories would widen your Japanese vocabulary and the audio would allow you to follow along to the words, expose you to correct Japanese pronunciation, and help you practice your listening comprehension.

If you need more help with learning Japanese, please visit www.talkinjapanese.com.

Cheers and best of luck to you!

Talk In Japanese Team

音声をダウンロードする方法に関する説明

INSTRUCTIONS ON HOW TO DOWNLOAD THE AUDIO

Please take note that the audio are in MP3 format and need to be accessed online. No worries though; it's quite easy! Simply follow the instructions below. It will teach you the steps on where and how to download this book's accompanying audio.

On your computer, smartphone, iphone/ipad or tablet, go to this link:

http://talkinjapanese.com/mp3-japanese-stories/

The link will give you two options:

1. a direct link where you can listen to the audio and download it immediately, and
2. a link to download the files via Dropbox.

Take note that if you want an easier way to access the files using any type of device (including iOS), choose the direct link option. But if you are a Dropbox user who wants to access the files on your Dropbox account, you can also use the Dropbox option as an alternative.

Here's how to download using the two different options:

Method 1: Get the audio via Direct Link

- In the link provided above, choose the DIRECT LINK option.
- Proceed to the page and listen to the audio directly or download it to any device.

Method 2: Download the audio files via Dropbox

- After selecting the Dropbox option on the page, you will see the MP3 files saved in a Dropbox folder.
- Locate the DOWNLOAD button on the Dropbox folder or save it to your own Dropbox so you can access the audio on connected devices.
- The files you have downloaded would be saved in a .zip file. Simply extract these files from the .zip folder, save to your computer or copy to your preferred devices. If your smartphone or tablet has a zip file extractor, you can download it immediately onto your device.

Do you have any problems downloading the audio? If you do, feel free to send an email to contact@talkinjapanese.com. we'll do our best to assist you, but we would greatly appreciate if you thoroughly review the instructions first.

Thank you. Merci.

ABOUT TALK IN JAPANESE
TALK IN JAPANESEについて

TalkInJapanese.com believes that Japanese can be learned almost painlessly with the help of a learning habit. Through its website and the books and audiobooks that it offers, Japanese language learners are treated to high quality materials that are designed to keep them motivated until they reach their language learning goals.

Keep learning Japanese and enjoy the learning process with books and audio from Talk In Japanese.

Printed in Poland
by Amazon Fulfillment
Poland Sp. z o.o., Wrocław